Faces of
Tyranny

An American
Finds Faith and
Freedom Behind
the Crumbling
Iron Curtain

MJ HAYNER

A wholly owned subsidary of **TBN**

Faces of Tyranny: An American Finds Faith and Freedom Behind the Crumbling Iron Curtain

Trilogy Christian Publishers A Wholly Owned Subsidiary of Trinity Broadcasting Network

2442 Michelle Drive Tustin, CA 92780

For information about special discounts for bulk purchases, please contact Trilogy Christian Publishing.

Manufactured in the United States of America
10 9 8 7 6 5 4 3 2 1
Library of Congress Cataloging-in-Publication Data is available.
ISBN: 978-1-63769-894-5
E-ISBN: 978-1-63769-895-2

Dedication

I am dedicating this book to my patient husband, Monty, who lovingly encouraged me to write this book. Also, to our wonderful children, Brian, Katie, Kristina, and Leighann, I love you more than I can say.

Acknowledgments

A special thank you to my friends, Linda, Sandy, Bridget, and Evelyn, and to my sisters, Joanne, Barbara, and Gail, who have been supportive to me as I wrote this book.

Table of Contents

Prologue 11

Flight to Vienna. 13

What Is Tyranny? 17

A Childhood Memory 25

Arrival in Vienna. 29

Historic Vienna 33

Background of The Velvet Revolution 39

The Velvet Revolution 45

Approaching the Border 49

Entering Czechoslovakia 53

The Angry Man from Chynice 57

The Nightmare from My Childhood. 65

Trauma on a Horse 71

An Angry Beating. 79

Moving to the Big Farm 81

Macro and Micro Versions of Tyranny 85

Entering Prague. 89

First Night in Prague. 101

My Wedding 105

The Birth of My Son. 113

Life on the Road 119

Back in Minneapolis. 125

Growing Tyranny in My Life 131

My Breakdown 135

Enlightenment. 141

Second Day in Prague. 149

The Physics Professor. 157

Prague University Students. 165

Individualism 169

New Idealism in Prague 171

Reflection on My Childhood. 175

Kathleen 181

Table of Contents

David. 185

Kristina 195

Moving Out of Minneapolis 199

Prelude to My Trip 203

Karlovy Vary. 209

The Minister of Transportation. 215

Bratislava 227

Trnava. 231

Hlohovec. 237

The Interviews 241

The Retired Nurse. 249

Evening with the Interpreter. 251

A Comparison of the Economies
     Between 1990 and 2019. 257

Going Home 265

Epilogue 271

Bibliography 273

About the Author. 279

Prologue

Tyranny is one of the dark powers that exist in our world. Our battle is not against people themselves but against the powers that want to control and destroy us through evil. Even a child knows that life is sometimes unfair and afflicted by various evils. Evil exists in a realm we do not see, yet its impact is apparent in our lives and in the lives of others in our world.

It is not my goal to judge anyone. Only God can judge the hearts of people. Since all have fallen short of perfection, we all live under the influence of evil, and it has sometimes had its way in our lives. However, tyranny can be overcome. In order to do that, just like in separating wheat from the chaff, truth must be found amidst the lies. Finding truth and then having the faith and courage to act on it is the recipe for defeating tyranny.

This is a true story of tyranny, masked by the faces and unique personalities of the oppressors it has invaded *and the overcomers who dared to defy it.*

Flight to Vienna

June 1990, over the Atlantic Ocean

It was early June 1990, just six months after the Velvet Revolution, the peaceful overthrow of the Communist government in Czechoslovakia. With rigid determination, I was working up courage to face a long airplane ride.

As I boarded my first flight from Minneapolis, Minnesota, to New York, I put my hand on the outside of the plane and quietly prayed, "Lord, please bring us safely to our destination." I did the same thing later when boarding a connecting flight to Vienna, Austria. I often prayed, as I unashamedly depended on God's grace for strength to face my fears. I have always had a fear of heights, and flying made me very nervous. What I didn't understand at the time was what a deep impact the stories of the people that I would soon meet would have on me. I realized much later that it was during this trip that I began the journey to truly face down the tyranny in my own life, and like those Czechoslovakians, I also yearned to be free.

Although I was looking forward to my independent study on the effect of communism on Czechoslovakia, I was also apprehensive. I had never been out of the country before this time, except for a canoe ride into Canada from the boundary waters of northern Minnesota when I was a teenager. The boundary waters were about forty miles from my childhood home in northern Minnesota and certainly didn't seem like a foreign trip. I had previously only been on a couple of short flights in my whole life, but now I was on a long flight across the ocean, taking me far away from my children. Not knowing exactly whom I would meet or what I would find behind the Iron Curtain, the dividing line between the free world and the communist world, my inner lack of confidence caused additional anxiety.

Though I would not be totally alone during the trip, as I was going to catch up with a tour group in Vienna before entering Czechoslovakia, this was the first time that I had done anything so daring. I believed in God, but I was still an insecure woman looking to learn about the world. Like a child who wants desperately to grow up and escape the confinements of youth, I wanted to be independent and do something worthwhile on my own. I was tired of being controlled by others in my life.

As the time dragged on during the flight, the excitement about my new adventure, the weariness of jet lag, and a fear of the unknown put me into an altered state of being. It was as if I was outside of my body, totally numb to my physical state, yet very aware of my surroundings. I sensed that I was going to experience something extraordinary, but I didn't know what awaited me after the long flight.

I imagined people with broken dreams living with scarce necessities, such as portrayed in the movie *Dr. Zhivago*, a movie made in 1965 about the communist revolution in Russia.[1] I remember one scene especially. When Dr. Zhivago, a doctor in Russia, returns to his home from the battlefield, he finds that his home has been looted and that strangers are living in it. Due to the communist takeover in 1917, he was allowed only one room for himself and his family in his own house. Most of his former possessions were either taken or destroyed.

As I wondered about the people that I would soon meet, I tried to remain calm. Even though I was scared, like walking alone through the woods at night to a mysterious cabin, I was determined to get to my destination. It was too late to turn back.

1 Wikipedia, 2021

What Is Tyranny?

This trip opened my eyes to the evils of imposed rule from one nation onto another. One definition of tyranny is cruel, unreasonable, or arbitrary use of power or control.[2] The spirit of tyranny invades the minds and hearts of oppressors, and many of them believe wholeheartedly that their ideas are right and good. However, since the oppressors' minds have been darkened by a sinister motive, such as vengeance or a desire for power, they may not see the evil that they are embracing. These ideas can start in the mind of one arrogant and sometimes bitter individual, like Adolf Hitler. Oftentimes, anger at events from childhood can drive the ruthlessness.

I also believe that many who have been oppressed become oppressors. Thinking vengeance is justice, and any bitterness is justified, people can open the door of their lives to evil and become new faces of tyranny, whether they are leaders of countries or heads of families. Punishing others under their rule, they do not realize that they have become just as evil as those who oppressed them. They also believe that the goal of righting any real or perceived wrongs justifies any nefarious tactics.

2 Bing, 2021

Tyranny's main weapons are lies, deception, and the blame game. Using these tools, tyranny impregnates fear, guilt, confusion, and hopelessness into its victims. Its goal is to gain power and destroy the well-being of society by killing the value of individuals within the society.

In a country, a powerfully persuasive and sinister leader can incite a group of weak-minded people into social action to further the leader's goals. As the ideas gain momentum through propaganda and by demonizing opponents, the tyrannical beast gains power within society. As the ideas become group-think, the beast gains more power and eventually has full control over individual expression of thought and will not allow even a small difference in opinion.

Many times, those who have a difference of opinion will cave in to the oppressors, hoping that appeasement will keep the beast from devouring them. An example of this was England's acquiescence of the Sudetenland in Czechoslovakia to Germany before World War II. English Prime Minister Chamberlain signed the 1938 Munich agreement with Adolf Hitler allowing Germany to invade Czechoslovakia with a promise from Hitler that he would not invade any other country in Europe.[3] The appeasement didn't work as Germany only gained more time to build its military might in order to invade more countries in Europe. Appeasement never works against the spirit of tyranny. It only gives it more power.

Tyranny can also invade family units. A household leader's unresolved anger at life experiences usually is the driving force behind opening the door to evil. Tyranny instills fear, low self-esteem, helplessness, and hopelessness into the family members under its control. The oppression usually comes in one or more of the following forms; child abuse, incest, and domestic violence.

Throughout the ages, people have lived under many tyrannical regimes, which usually included some form of a religious or political system. Most regimes have had a societal structure that included slavery and/or other various oppressive forms of class systems. There has never been a truly free system of government, mainly because without some form of control, society would be a lawless anarchy. However, there is an innate desire in all people to be free and valued within an ordered and fair society. I have never met an able-minded person that did not want freedom

3 Wikipedia, 2021

to accomplish their dreams, provide for their needs, and associate with like-minded people. The only time people give up any of these freedoms is by force or if they are enticed to exchange it for some sort of benefit or security promised. The latter can happen in a time of crisis.

An example of this was the rise of the Third Reich in Germany before World War II. Adolf Hitler, a well-known face of tyranny, promised the German people that they would rise out of the ashes and humiliation of World War I and become a prosperous, great nation again. The people fell for his lies and propaganda and elected him as their leader.

Hitler and Nazi propagandists took advantage of long-established German anti-Semitism. Jews were blamed for things such as robbing Germany of the benefits of the German people's hard work. The accusation came from an unsubstantiated rumor alleging that the Jews were the originators of the Russian Bolshevik Revolution in 1917.[4] Although it is true that the main proponent of communism, Karl Marx, was of Jewish lineage, he was not a practicing Jew. He was an atheist.

---

4 Wikipedia 2021

Hitler claimed that the three vices of Jewish Bolshevism were democracy, pacifism, and internationalism and that Jews were instrumental in the birth of communism.[5] One of Hitler's missions in the Nazi movement was to destroy this so-called Jewish Bolshevism. Like the communists, the tyrannical Nazis wanted full control over the world, but with only German elitists in charge. The official name of the Nazi party was the National Socialist German Worker's Party, which implies a socialistic agenda.

Playing the blame game, Hitler blamed the Jewish people for Germany's woes. After an onslaught of propaganda, the German people bought into Hitler's ideas. In just a few years, Hitler's government took away freedoms, massacred millions of people, and destroyed the German nation as well as many others. Czechoslovakia was one of the victims of Hitler's horrific lunacy. Sadly, after being liberated from Nazi rule, the country was again invaded and lived through another forty-plus years of tyranny under Soviet communist rule. In spite of any differing agendas in the two regimes, tyranny still reigned, and the result was destruction.

---

5 Id.

One of the most famous faces of tyranny in the twentieth century was a Soviet communist ruler named Joseph Stalin. He was well-known for turning on even his friends if it suited his goal of attaining and retaining iron-fisted power in the Soviet Union. His chief of police once said, implying that Stalin approved of the saying, "Show me the man, and I will show you the crime."[6] If Stalin saw someone as a threat to his power, he would find a way to destroy that person.

Stalin even assassinated loyal members of his own party. *The Great Terror*, which occurred between 1936 and 1938, is credited for killing more communists than Hitler and Mussolini combined during World War II. One estimate of the total death toll during this purge was approximately twenty million people.[7] Stalin used very unreasonable, cruel, and arbitrary power in subduing and controlling the citizens of the Soviet Union from 1922 until his death in 1953.

The inevitable outcome of tyrannical power is the destruction of the society or institution that it has invaded. It crushes the individual spirit within the people it rules. Like cancer in the body, tyranny

6 Savage, 2018
7 Wikipedia, 2021

grows and emaciates the society it has infected, and the results are hopelessness, dependence, murder, genocide, social decay, and poverty. Tyranny sears the conscience of the oppressors and begets fear in the oppressed. At the same time, it kills self-worth, kindness, ingenuity, and dignity in individuals.

Tyranny can arise in many human institutions. It ruled over the people of Czechoslovakia, and in my life, it ruled in my own family. One of my earliest memories is one of tyranny.

A Childhood Memory

June 1956, Northern Minnesota Dairy Farm

It was an early summer morning in 1956. I was three and a half years old. My mother had sent me outside to join my father in the barn at our small dairy farm in northern Minnesota. After a short walk to the barn, I climbed up a couple of cement stairs which led to a large, white barn door. I opened the door latch and peered inside. The barn was somewhat dark, but after my eyes focused, I saw about seven black and white cows lined up in stalls on one side of the barn. The cement floor had a gutter placed strategically behind the cows in case they had the urge to defecate. A pungent odor of hay mixed with manure hung in the air.

As I quietly stepped into the barn, I saw my dad next to one of the docile but mooing cows. My father was of average height, dark-haired, and very handsome. He was athletically built and very energetic. My mom once talked about their first meeting, which occurred at a military dance after World War II. She claimed that my dad was so handsome that she immediately fell in love with him. They were married about six months later.

After entering the barn, I watched as my dad busily set up the milking machines for the morning milking. Although I didn't know how the process worked at the time, I would learn later that after the electricity was turned on, the milking machines would intermittently squeeze each cow's udders to extract the milk. The milk would flow from the milking machines, go through a pipe-way of glass tubes that were attached to the walls of the barn, and finally enter a large metal container that would keep the milk cool until the milk truck arrived.

After a couple of seconds of watching my father, I turned my focus to the black and white cow towering above me in its stall. It was at least five times larger than my dad, which seemed gigantic from a three-year-old's perspective. I quickly noticed that all of the cows intermittently swished their tails at the buzzing flies surrounding them. It was much different than a windshield wiper's regular movement. Each sudden tail-slapping movement startled me, and I soon cried out to my dad. Since my dad still had to finish his task, he placed me in a corner of the barn away from the cows. I quietly stood there while keeping my eyes on the cows. Eventually, my dad finished his tasks, flipped a switch, and the milking began.

I was fascinated as I listened to the humming of the milking machines and watched the milk flow through the glass tubes on the barn wall before entering the large milk container. My fixation on the milking was soon disturbed when a stranger entered the barn. I quickly turned my focus to the stranger. The man was about my father's height and wore the same olive-green farmer's outfit. With a smile on his face, he walked toward my father and shook his hand. Soon, they were involved in a serious conversation. They spoke to each other as if I wasn't there.

Feeling insecure from being ignored, I ran up to my father and hastily hugged what I thought was his knee. I immediately heard my father and the stranger begin to laugh. I looked up at their amused faces and shockingly realized that I had grabbed the wrong man's leg. Scared and ashamed, I quickly pulled back from the stranger and began to cry. However, my dad did not comfort me. Instead, after the laughter ended, he ignored me again and finished his conversation with the man. I sobbed to myself for a few more minutes until the man left. Still crying, I ran back to my dad, hoping that he would pick me up. I was confused and upset, wondering why my dad was ignoring me.

My father must have been irritated with my crying and clinginess. He may have been stressed because of an issue with the man who had just left. He did not pick me up. Instead, he shut off the milking machines and started to leave the barn. Afraid of being left alone in the barn, I ran after him. I was now wailing as I frantically followed him, but he didn't turn around. When I almost caught up to him, he swung his arm back at me as if he was trying to get away from me. His fist hit me square in my middle, and I went flying backward. I don't remember landing, but my head must have hit hard on the barn door. When I came back into consciousness, I was sitting in shock with my back up against the barn door. My father was gone. I don't think that he even realized what he had done. I don't know how long I sat in front of the barn, but I know that after the shock eased, I felt a painful sense of abandonment and worthlessness.

I do not have a memory of what transpired next, but as a result of this traumatic incident, I did not trust my father anymore. I was afraid of him. As I grew up, my dignity would be further eroded as I suffered more pain in my childhood.

Arrival in Vienna

June 1990, Vienna, Austria

After nervously deplaning in Vienna, Austria, I approached the line to go through customs. Other people leaving the plane seemed relaxed, at least in comparison to me, as if landing in another country was usual for them. I kept any anxious feelings in check, mostly by assuring myself that God would protect and guide me. I was also very tired since I didn't sleep well on the overnight flight from New York to Vienna. The jet lag subdued some of the nervousness.

Getting through customs was uneventful, but as I turned a corner in the airport to go to baggage claim, a jolt of shock went through me as I saw heavily armed soldiers standing guard throughout the airport. Tall and muscular, each had on a dark uniform with a beret on their head and held what seemed to be a huge machine gun. At that moment, my naivety about world tensions was annihilated. My heart began to beat rapidly as I stopped and stared at the soldiers. It dawned on me that the world near the Iron Curtain, the border between the Soviet Union and the free world, was on high alert. At any moment, war could erupt. Only the year before, in May of 1989, Hungary had declared its independence from the Soviet Union and opened its border to Austria as it broke through the Iron Curtain. Among the many Hungarians crossing the border, thousands of East Germans had also fled through this open border.[8] Austria was on guard as the Soviet Union could come down hard on them for accepting the refugees.

After walking cautiously through the airport, I arrived at baggage claim and collected my bag. Suitcases with rollers were uncommon in 1990, so as I picked up my bag, I was glad that I had packed light. As my eyes furtively looked around for danger, I nervously walked toward the airport exit area to find the professor who would be my tour group leader.

When I reached the vestibule, I tried to calm my anxious thoughts. I didn't know what the professor looked like, and I was worried that he might not show up. Thankfully, my concerns were allayed when I saw a middle-aged man holding a small, white sign with my name on it. As I greeted the graying, short, and stout professor, my heart palpitations started to ease. I was so thankful to be finally united with the travel group, but I was still a little nervous about meeting so

8 Wikipedia, 2021

many new people.

As we walked outside into the bright, warm sunshine, the rays from the sun penetrated both my body and soul. The smell of fresh June grass growing in the nearby field reminded me of home. I felt a momentary wave of homesickness wash over me since I already missed my children. As I looked around, I saw a tranquil, green, farm-like country partially surrounded by small dark mountains. I had been expecting to see an ancient, bustling city all around me when I left the airport. Instead, the city of Vienna was located a few miles away.

I followed the professor to the parked tour bus, located across the street from the airport. It was not far from the terminal. After shyly boarding the tour bus, I met my companion travelers. Much to my surprise, I saw only a small group of about a dozen people. I was supposed to join an economic forum, but right then, I realized that I was traveling with a tourist group. Even though I was dismayed, I decided not to say anything to the professor and try to make the most of the trip. In hindsight, though, I was exactly where I was supposed to be. I was supposed to be with this particular group of people to learn what I was supposed to learn.

God had a plan, but I didn't understand it yet.

Being somewhat introverted, I only got to know some of my companion travelers. I did enjoy the company of an anesthesiologist from Seattle, his wife, and their two children. I did not know it at the time, but they would introduce me to their cousin in Prague, who was a physics professor at one of the oldest universities in the world, Charles University. His story of courage during the Velvet Revolution, the impetus for Czechoslovakia's freedom from communism, would inspire me greatly.

Historic Vienna

We stayed in Vienna for two days. In 1990, Vienna was a free, prosperous, ancient city located on the Danube River. The city was first established during the Roman Empire, which explains the combinations of Gothic, Rococo, Baroque, and other more modern architecture styles visible in the buildings.

On the first day, we visited the 1,441 roomed Schönbrunn palace where a young Mozart had entertained the Holy Roman Emperor, Joseph II. The Rococo-styled palace had been completed and remodeled in the middle of the eighteenth century and had been the summer home for the Hapsburg ruling family.[9] Surrounded by many lush gardens on 500 acres of land, including a famous maze on the grounds, the palace grounds are also inhabited by large, intricate statues of mythological deities and virtues. They are situated along the walkways and seem to be guarding the palace. It is a large palace, filled with many rooms having different themes. They are all decorated with gilded walls and furniture, opulent furnishings, paintings, and tapestries.

---

9 Wikipedia, 2021

Schönbrunn Palace

As we walked through the palace, my mind went back in time and imagined some of the moments that must have taken place in each room. I thought about what it must have been like to hear the young Mozart play piano for the royal family. I imagined the young daughters who had once lived in the palace laughing and teasing each other while dressing for the many dinners and other festive occasions that had occurred at the palace.

I was most impressed by the paintings of the daughters of Maria Theresa, seven in all, including her most famous daughter, Marie Antionette. Maria

Theresa was the mother of Joseph II and was co-ruler with him until her death in 1780.[10] The paintings were displayed on the walls of the Children's room. Strangely, the daughters posed in the paintings all seemed to look very much alike. A comment was made to that effect, and the tour guide glibly responded that they looked eerily similar because the painter did not want to offend any of the sisters by making one appear more beautiful than another.

On the second day, after a short bus ride from our hotel, we disembarked and walked to Mozart's apartment, where he had lived with his family in the heart of Vienna between 1784 and 1787.[11] The sun's bright rays and the cool morning breeze encouraged me to make the most of my day. Since I do not like being in crowds, the lack of large groups of tourists enhanced my excitement about my new adventure.

Mozart's apartment is located east of the most prominent church in Vienna, St. Stephen's Cathedral, which we visited next. The huge cathedral was constructed in the fourteenth century in Gothic and Romanesque style.[12] I had never seen such an old, huge and magnificent church before this time. The majestic

10 Wikipedia, 2021
11 Id.
12 Id.

cathedral is full of marbled statues, golden altars, monuments and is surrounded by huge stained-glass windows. The stained-glass windows towering above me gave me vertigo, almost causing me to fall to the floor.

There are eighteen altars in the cathedral, but the main altar, the High Altar, was exquisite. It depicts in gold the stoning of St. Stephen. There was so much to see in every nook and cranny of the cathedral that it almost diminished the attention that the main altar deserved. The view was overwhelming. My greedy eyes could not stay on each unique artifact very long before wanting to move on to the next.

As I first walked along the narrow, cobblestone streets of Vienna, a feeling of awe hit me as I realized how much history had taken place in the city. It felt as if I had been transported back in time. In amazement, my eyes gobbled up every sight in front of me. The old buildings seemed almost unreal to me. In the United States, a building is considered old if it is a hundred years old, but in Vienna, that same building would be considered new.

After entering and walking through Mozart's five-room apartment, I came upon the room where Mozart did his composing. I was struck by its simplicity since there was very little furniture or paintings on the wall. I was almost immediately drawn to a copy of one of Mozart's compositions laying on a desk. From what I was told, it was in this room where he composed *The Marriage of Figaro*. Having taken piano lessons as a child, I marveled at his genius and thought to myself, how could anyone write such a complex musical composition by using just his mind, a piano, and a pen?

That night at the hotel, I wondered what the next day would hold. I was excited but still somewhat tense, not knowing what I would encounter. I had already learned about the events leading up to the Velvet Revolution, but I wasn't totally prepared to immerse myself into the country of Czechoslovakia at such a perilous time in history. I prayed that God would grant me peace and wisdom in whatever I might encounter. I eventually fell asleep.

Background of The Velvet Revolution

The Czechoslovak Socialist Republic had been established in 1948, after the liberation of the country from Nazi Germany by the Allied troops. The country stayed a Marxist-Leninist state as part of the Eastern Soviet Bloc of nations until April of 1990.[13] The other nations in the Eastern Bloc were East Germany, Poland, Hungary, Romania, Bulgaria, and Albania.[14] The Communist Party's main purpose was to spread communism throughout the remaining civilized world. This aggression also prompted the Cold War with the West and established what was called the Iron Curtain, the dividing line between Eastern and Western Europe. Establishing satellite nations like Czechoslovakia was a big step forward for the goals of the party.

After the introduction of Perestroika reforms in 1985 by the Soviet Union's leader, Mikhail Gorbachev, more freedoms were finally allowed behind the Iron Curtain. Those freedoms were not allowed in Czechoslovakia. Gustav Husak, the dictator of Czechoslovakia at the time, decided to ban the reforms. This angered

13 Wikipedia, 2021
14 Id.

the students and professors at the universities. By 1988, organized student demonstrations were demanding change. These demonstrations went on for about another year.[15]

Finally, in November of 1989, just a couple of weeks after the fall of the Berlin Wall, the rule of communism in Czechoslovakia also came crashing down.[16] Even though the revolution was successful, the country was still under some control by the communist leaders. Czechoslovakia would not fully be a free, independent nation until the full transfer of power took place in June of 1990, very soon after my visit.[17]

Prior to my trip, I had been watching on television the news and the events leading up to the 1989 fall of the Iron Curtain. I watched President Reagan give his famous speech at the Berlin wall in June of 1987 asking the Soviet Union's General Secretary, Mikhail Gorbachev, to tear down the Berlin wall. The wall was part of the Iron Curtain. It separated free West Berlin from communist-controlled East Berlin. Reagan's speech was electrifying. As I noticed the overwhelmingly positive reaction from the Germans to the speech, I sensed that something historic was about to

15 Id.
16 Id.
17 University of Central Arkansas, 2021

happen. I became much more interested in watching the news and monitoring our nation's political pulse. Before that time, I was not very interested in politics.

In 1988, because I was studying economics in college, I began to understand the connection between the economy and politics. I became much more interested in studying the effects of differing ideologies and the impact those views had on a nation's economy and social structures.

Ideology is the groundwork of people's behavior. It is the foundation of what people believe is right and good, so it forms society's norms. It is the basic element behind the formation of law and order in society, and it determines a country's values. For example, hard work and success are valued in a capitalistic society. People who are talented, skilled, and work hard are rewarded. The best in business, sports, and entertainment are honored, applauded, and made wealthy by others in society.

The biggest issue for capitalism is keeping the playing field fair and equal. Money and power go hand-in-hand, so laws must be implemented and enforced to prevent those with a great amount of money from abusing others. A moral code underneath those laws is the compass for keeping society fair. In the United States, the moral code was originally based on Judeo-Christian ethics.

In a communist society, equity, or equal outcome, is valued. As a result, ordinary people tend to avoid excellence. Sometimes an athlete, a space hero, or an entertainer receives notoriety, but it is rare. Since everyone is supposed to have equal outcomes, no one wants to be a stand-out. Instead, hard work and individual successes are discouraged, so there is little motivation to build wealth. It is the reason that innovation is seriously lacking in a communist society. All major breakthroughs in technology, such as the cell phone or personal computer, didn't occur under communism; they occurred in a capitalistic society.

The economic pie, or the wealth produced by a nation, is not one sized. It grows and shrinks based on the nation's productivity and resources. The ideology of a nation undergirds the laws and norms of society, but it also determines its level of productivity. A free, capitalistic nation allows for more self-determination. People can choose their own occupation and even be their own boss. In this environment, workers have a chance to live the life of their own choosing.

Greater productivity in a capitalist system stems from using natural resources more efficiently. Waste is reduced because the people have skin in the game. Through private ownership and by offering individual rewards for productivity, wealth increases because there is a motivation to use natural resources wisely and for the best outcome. Since a free nation is a more productive nation than a communist nation, it will always have the most wealth.

Communism promotes atheism and statism, so its ideology is not based on an outside moral code, such as Christianity, Islam, or Buddhism. It is arbitrary and based on the state's progressive or evolving ideas about what is right and good. The state becomes its own moral compass. Its rules and laws can change easily based on the whims of those in power. Without an external moral compass, as the saying goes, "Absolute power corrupts absolutely."

Ideology also fuels political beliefs, and those applied political beliefs form the economic and social structures of a nation. As I started learning more about the Czechoslovakian people's reaction to the imposed economic and social structures under communist rule, I began to admire this small Eastern

European nation and the people who fought for their freedoms.

A six-week period, between November 17 and December 29, 1989, brought about the nonviolent overthrow of the communist government desired by the students and eventually the whole country of Czechoslovakia. The Czechs do not seem to like the moniker, *Velvet Revolution*, preferring to call the time the *November Events*. However, the *Velvet Revolution* is what the rest of the world calls that period of time in Czechoslovakia.

The Velvet Revolution

In 1990, even though many years had passed since World War II, Czechoslovakians still had strong feelings about Germany and the previous Nazi rule. Every year in Prague, a memorial rally is held for a young medical student, Jan Opletal, who was shot and killed by the Nazi police in 1939 at an anti-Nazi protest march. The rally is held yearly on November 17th to remember this student.[18] His memory became the symbol of Czechoslovakian resistance to the Nazi's tyrannical regime.

Using a German dictionary and my limited knowledge of the German language, I tried to communicate with a couple of the first people that I met in Prague. A student frowned and shook her head at me, implying that German was not a preferred language. I was amazed that the people still felt so strongly about the oppression that had happened so long ago. But tyranny leaves a lasting impression, especially if the population is still being oppressed, even if the oppression is done by a different dictatorship.

---

18 Wikipedia, 2020

During the first protest of the Velvet Revolution in Prague on November 17, 1989, student organizers demanded the government's resignation using banners and posters. Just like a crack in a dam before it breaks, this first protest was the first crack in the wall of communism in Czechoslovakia. Very soon, the crack grew larger with the formation of the Civic Forum. The Civic Forum was a unified group of dissident leaders from various occupations. It formed less than forty-eight hours after the first protest.[19] The Civic Forum was led by playwriter and future president Vaclav Havel. It demanded the resignation of the communist leaders and the release of political prisoners.

Vaclav Havel had determined that strikes would be the most effective tool against the government, so he organized a general strike to occur all across Czechoslovakia on November 27, 1989. The crack in the wall of communism got even larger when trade union members decided to join the movement. Havel and the Civic Forum then planned more mass demonstrations throughout the country to openly express their displeasure with the communist government. They also wanted to advertise the November 27th general strike.[20] As a result, new rallies took place in cities all

19 Wikipedia, 2021
20 Wikipedia, 2021

across Czechoslovakia. At the same time, the universities and entertainment venues were being used to design new local and national government policies.

Two days prior to the November 27th strike, even larger protests occurred in Prague, each drawing a crowd of nearly 750,000 people. These protests paved the way for meetings between the Civic Forum and the communist Prime Minister, Ladislav Adamec. In those meetings, Adamec would eventually guarantee that no violence would be used against citizens.[21]

At noon, on November 27, 1989, the strike began. Expressing unanimous support for the Civic Forum, about seventy-five percent of the population participated in the two-hour general strike. Offices, businesses, and factories all throughout the country totally stopped work for two hours.[22] The strike was the final break in the wall of communism. Along with the earlier protests, the strike had successfully impressed on the communist regime that the Czechoslovakian people would no longer obey their oppressive rule. The Republic of Czechoslovakia was then reborn, and freedom for the Czechoslovakian people had become a reality at last. Vaclav Havel was elected President in

---

21 Id.
22 Id.

December of 1989 and then again in July of 1990.[23]

If it hadn't been for the bravery of the student leaders, the Velvet Revolution would have never happened. They created the first chip in the wall of communism in their country. Even though Czechoslovakia was not the first nation to rebel against communism and cut through the Iron Curtain, it still took immense courage to stand up and be the first in their own country to defy the tyranny of the communist regime.

I would soon experience firsthand the tension that the country was facing during this crucial moment in history. Unbeknownst to me, I would also soon be meeting one of the student leaders in Prague.

---

23 Wikipedia, 2020

Approaching the Border

June 1990, The Border between Austria and Czechoslovakia

On the third day of my trip, the tour bus traveled north towards Bohemia, a historical region in western Czechoslovakia, and the small village of Chynice, located in the central-western part of Czechoslovakia. I felt more secure approaching the border, knowing that I was with a tour group with pre-planned stops and places to stay.

Along the way, I quietly chit-chatted with the blond and blue-eyed children of the anesthesiologist. Even though they were both still in grade school, we had an engaging conversation about Seattle and their school. The adults all seemed preoccupied with their own thoughts, most likely thinking nervously about crossing the border. There was reason for concern about entering Czechoslovakia in June of 1990, as we would be one of the first tour groups to enter the country after the Velvet Revolution. Getting to know the charming boy and girl from Seattle eased some tension for me.

The people of Czechoslovakia were experiencing intense nervousness in June of 1990. The Czechoslovakian people had strong memories of the Prague Spring when the country first tried to free themselves of communism. At that time, the Soviet Union and other Eastern Bloc nation's armies had invaded Czechoslovakia to stop the potential revolution and return the country to pure communism. The people were afraid that a similar crackdown could occur again after the Velvet Revolution.

The Prague Spring was a period of political protest in Czechoslovakia. It began on January 5, 1968, when reformist Alexander Dubcek was elected First Secretary of the Communist Party of Czechoslovakia. It continued until August 21, 1968, when the Soviet Union and other Warsaw Pact members invaded the country to squelch the reforms. Even though Dubcek was a communist, he was considered to be too liberal by the hard-liners in Moscow. After the invasion, they forced him to resign.[24]

The memory of the 1968 Soviet crackdown caused understandable tensions amongst the Czechoslovakian people because a similar invasion orchestrated by the Soviet Union could easily happen again.

24 Wikipedia, 2021

In June of 1990, my tour group and I were entering Czechoslovakia during the time period of the transition of power from a communist-run government to a newly formed democratic government after the Velvet Revolution. Our nervousness about entering the country was very valid. Even though the Iron Curtain had lost its dark and strangling power over the people, a veil of communist control still lingered, so our nervousness about entering the country was very valid. Communists still flexed some muscular power over the people since communist soldiers still acted as the country's police for three more years. Communist soldiers would also be checking our passports as we entered the country, and I would soon meet face-to-face with one of them.

Entering Czechoslovakia

Upon approaching the border between Austria and Czechoslovakia, I saw a checkpoint ahead of us. A small guard station stood alongside the tar-paved road. A couple of guards were standing in the road just ahead of us. We would not be able to drive into Czechoslovakia until our passports were checked and approved. Even though there were a few soldiers at the checkpoint, only one approached the bus as it came to a stop. The professor, sitting in the front seat of the bus, asked us to have our passports ready. Soon the bus stopped, and the bus driver opened the door.

Tension gripped me as I heard the soldier's black boots bang on the metal steps as he boarded the bus. While he stood in front of the professor, I sized him up as he momentarily took stock of the professor.

The soldier was in his early thirties, tall and thin, and he wore a dark uniform. A gun was inserted into a side holster. As apprehension filled the air, the soldier spoke quietly but firmly to the professor, our tour guide. The professor didn't translate what the guard said but instead motioned to us to send him our passports. The passports were then silently passed up the aisle of the bus to the professor, who handed them to the guard.

The guard took the passports and began the process of validating them. Without speaking directly to any of us, he sternly walked down the aisle, stopping to very intently look at each passport and its matching face. When he stopped to look at me, I felt very intimidated, as it seemed like he was memorizing my face. It also seemed to me that he spent more time on me than on the others, even though that was unlikely true. His look was questioning as if he wasn't sure that my passport was really mine. I was glad that I had not changed my hair length since getting the passport. After what seemed to be many minutes, the guard finally moved on and finished his process. With a slight nod, he gave the passports back to the professor and exited the bus.

We were not immediately waved through the checkpoint. Still feeling rattled by the experience with the guard, I bit my lip as I watched him walk toward the other guards standing near the checkpoint gate. As I watched the guards conversing with each other for a few more minutes, I had a fearful thought that maybe they were even considering taking one or more of us into custody. After a few minutes, though, the gate was opened, and a guard motioned our bus through. As we drove into the country, we all breathed a collective a sigh of relief. Lighter-hearted conversations soon began.

As we drove further into Czechoslovakia, I started noticing changes in the landscape. The slightly hilly summer countryside reminded me of early summer farmlands in central Minnesota. Green forests sometimes interrupted the view of the farms as I watched the scenery from my bus window. Some of the farm fields had been planted, and I could see small plants peeking out of each row in the fields. The sights were periodically interrupted by bumps from potholes along the way, so I assumed that road repair was seriously needed.

Eventually, it dawned on me what *wasn't* there. Very little traffic existed. I remember passing a couple of trucks on our drive, but I saw no passenger cars that are common on major highways in the United States. I found out later that owning a car was only for the communist elite. Minimizing travel for the average Czechoslovakian appeared to help the elite control the masses.

Most people lived, worked, and died in the same area that they were born, so bicycles, local buses or trains, or walking were their main means of transportation. When I was asked by a man in one of the cities that we visited, "How many cars do you own?" He was shocked when I answered, "Two." He commented that I must be very rich, but I didn't tell him that I was poor compared to many people in the United States, nor did I tell him that both of our vehicles were old and a bit run-down. It would have been rude to do so, so I just smiled and didn't say anything else. Later, I realized that I was rich, compared to many of the people that I met in Czechoslovakia. The poor in America are richer than the average person living under communism.

The Angry Man from Chynice

June 1990, Bohemian Village of Chynice, Czecho-slovakia

A couple of hours after entering Czechoslovakia, our tour bus arrived at our first destination, the village of Chynice in the region of Bohemia. The small town is located not too far from Prague, the capital of Czecho-slovakia. After we drove down the empty, winding street towards the center of the village, we came to the village square. In the square was a monument com-memorating the beloved sons of the village who were killed in World War I. Historically, Czechoslovakian town squares were the main area for commerce and also locations for churches and memorials.

The village was in very poor shape, as many of the one-story, stone, and wooden buildings were desper-ately in need of repair. There were broken windows, sagging roofs, and rotting wood. Disrepair would be a common sight in Czechoslovakia. The village lacked color, except for an occasional flower bed, as the buildings hadn't been painted in a long time. In contrast to the gloomy condition of the town, the sun was shining brightly. I felt a cool, early summer morning breeze as we disembarked from the bus.

We visited two homes in Chynice. The first home contained an elderly mother and her sixty-year-old daughter. The visit had been prearranged by the professor.

As the professor knocked on the door, we stood quietly behind him. The women lived in a dilapidated hut that had substandard plumbing. There was no bathroom, only a sink in the back of the room and an outhouse in the backyard. Instead of glass, cloth tapestries covered the windows. The old mother was sick, and neither of them spoke English, which was to be expected as English had been a banned language.

After the professor knocked on the door, the younger woman slowly opened her door. The professor greeted and then introduced her to the rest of us. He then asked in the Czech language for the younger woman to tell her story. The woman began to speak, pausing only to allow the professor time to interpret what she was saying. Translated by the professor turned tour guide, we learned that they were glad for the coming new government, led by Vaclav Havel.

Havel had previously been a social activist and play-writer, and due to his anti-communist beliefs and writings before the Velvet Revolution, he had also spent time in prison under the communist regime.

While the younger woman stood in the doorway doing all of the talking, the white-haired, old mother sat behind her in a rocking chair. She would periodically nod in agreement. They both wore long, peasant-style dresses. Their hair was folded neatly into a bun and wrapped by a multi-colored head kerchief. The inside of the home looked clean but sparsely furnished.

We were not invited into the house since there was no room for all of us inside the small hut. As our tour guide stood by the open door, we stood behind him on their unkempt lawn. A freshly plowed field sat behind their home. The scent of the dewy, green grass mixed with the smell of manure in the fertilized fields reminded me of the cow pastures and fields of my childhood farm.

The women did not seem very bitter about their living conditions, but they did angrily say that when the communist government took over after World War II, the communist enforcers also took away the father's means of making a living as a carpenter. His woodworking tools had been sent to Russia, and he was forced to become a truck driver.

I was shocked by their story. I couldn't imagine a government taking away a piano from a pianist, paintbrushes from a painter, or tools from a carpenter and then be told to be a truck driver, a ditch digger, or something else unrelated to one's skills, dreams, or individual goals.

As I empathized with the women, I internally evaluated the situation and thought, tyrannical rule leads to hopelessness, anger, and broken dreams in individuals. The people then become discouraged, which then affects their individual productivity, creativity, and ingenuity. The result is not only great anger and resentment toward the rulers but also incompetency in the assigned work. Incompetency and resentment then breed unproductivity in those individuals, who then provide substandard products and services. These chain reactions birthed the poverty and social decay that I saw all around me in Chynice.

As our conversation was ending, the women asked us to talk to another man who lived down the street to hear his story. We said our goodbyes to the women, and the professor thanked them profusely. Then, we walked down the narrow street toward the old man's home. The professor knocked on his door.

The man we visited was a large, gray-haired, and wrinkled man. I guessed that he was probably in his seventies. He appeared to have once been a muscular man. After we made our introductions, he gruffly told us his story. He had been a farmer with forty-five acres of land before the communist takeover. Afterward, he was left with only one acre and one small building. The bigger house and farm buildings were ransacked by the communists and then left empty to rot. Eventually, gypsies moved in.

Ironically, gypsies were considered to be a lower class of people, even though only one class of people supposedly existed under communism. Gypsies were labeled as thieves, even though theft was a common occurrence in the communist system. For example, it was a widely accepted practice to take whatever was desired from a place of employment. I chuckled at the thought that anyone could be called a thief since, in Karl Marx's envisioned utopia, all people share property and wealth.[25]

---

25 Hoyt, 2021

The disgruntled man's home was a small, two-roomed building. I was appalled at the degrading poverty displayed in his surroundings. It was dark inside because the main room only had a couple of small windows. There were no panes of glass nor screens to keep the bugs or elements from entering his home. The door to his home was also missing. Besides trying to adjust my ears to the gruffness of the old man's voice, I was occasionally distracted by flies buzzing in and out of his home. I thought about what it must be like in the winter when the cold winds came. I was sure that he would have to cover the windows with something during the cold months to keep from freezing to death. His sparse furnishings were also very old. After he let us into his home, he went to sit in his only chair while we stood and listened to his story.

Angry Man from Chynice

The man angrily expressed his humiliation at losing most of his property to the gypsies. He was very hateful toward the communists. When he was halfway through his story, I vividly remember him angrily shouting in the Czech language. When the professor translated, I found out that the man had exclaimed, "The communists should all be hung!"

The old man was bitter that little had been done to avenge him and others like him. He angrily made his case by saying, "The punishments meted out to the communists in the village were too mild. The police had been too sympathetic toward the communists. They should have at least been put in prison and not just fired from their jobs." He had much vengeance in his heart, and I believe that he would have also become an oppressor if he had been given power. I felt empathy for him, though, because he had lost so much more than just his land and his buildings. Because he was the victim of tyranny, he had lost his dignity and purpose. I was sad for him as he had lived a life of anger and despair for so many years.

As I pondered the experience of meeting these people as we left the village to head towards Prague, I realized that Karl Marx was at least right about the value of work. When the means of production were confiscated by the communists, the people became depressed, purposeless, and unproductive. However, the communist government fell way short in accomplishing another Marxist goal of bringing *meaningful* work to the people of Czechoslovakia. The government not only stole the means of production from the people, like the woodworking tools and farmland, but they also took away the people's beloved professions.

My mind then wandered away from thinking about the angry man. It drifted into thinking about my earlier life. I felt a connection to the people that I had just met since I had also been controlled, discouraged, and almost robbed of my own dignity and purpose. I realized that power in the hands of self-serving or angry people deeply hurts the lives under its control.

The Nightmare from My Childhood

Winter of 1966, Northern Minnesota Family Farm

I awoke with a start. My heart was wildly pounding. It was still dark, and I was very afraid. The clothes in the closet all seemed like figures ready to jump out at me. But mostly, I was afraid of my father. I had awoken again to the same place in the dream that I always do. I was standing by the barn gate screaming, "No!" The cows had turned around and were running back to the pasture after I had herded them to the front of the barn gate.

As I slowly came back to reality, I thought of the day ahead of me. I would take the early bus to school for band practice, but I did not have to get up early to milk the cows anymore. At age thirteen in 1966, I was now the eldest of five children as both of my older sisters had left to go to college. We had moved to a bigger farm a couple of years ago. My parents had sold the smaller farm, located just down the road from the larger farm, along with the milking cows. Even though my parents had sold the dairy farm, I would relive the cow milking days in my nightmare for years to come.

Summer of 1960, Northern Minnesota Dairy Farm

In 1960, when my younger sister, Gail, and I were six and seven years old, respectively, we fetched the cows on foot in the late spring, summer, and early fall. We continued the chore for two more years. We were bigger in size than our two older sisters had been at the same age, so I believe that my parents thought that we were mature enough to do more difficult chores than our age should allow. Being the older child and feeling more responsible for the task, pent-up anxiety in me eventually reached a saturation point. I believe that this anxiety caused the recurring nightmare. It also created in me an anxious determination to succeed at any assigned task. Failure meant punishment for me. If I did fail, which sometimes did happen, I would feel frustration, fear, and tremendous self-condemnation. I would then await the punishment that my parents might dole out to me.

The pasture at the small farm was composed of multiple acres of meadows and woods, with a small lake located in its center. From the barn, we would walk down a sloping gulley to a shallow, clear creek, where purple violets and blue forget-me-not flowers grew alongside the cold, clear water during the spring and summer. Before approaching the pasture, we would have to navigate through dark-green ferns growing amidst tall pine and birch trees on both sides of the creek. A fresh, clean scent would hang in the air as we moved to the rhythm of trickling water in the shallow, rock-filled creek. We would look for larger rocks to jump on in the middle of the creek to avoid stepping in the water while crossing over it.

Once in a while, we would hear a lynx screech an eerie sound, which would ignite some fear in us. Occasionally, I would disturb a partridge sitting in the brush, which would startle me as it flew away when I almost stepped on it. As long as it was still daylight and not storming, I wasn't too afraid of my surroundings. I was more afraid of my parents than the risks of nature, so I was tensely determined to succeed in bringing the cows home for milking.

Before my younger sister, Gail, and I walked into the field where the cows usually were, we would find sticks near the woods for cattle prods. Then we would pick a side behind the cows and begin to herd them home. The cows would normally be willing to go back to the barn to avoid the pain of engorgement from not getting milked. Once in a while, we would have some difficulties.

One time, during the first year of our herding days, we found ourselves in a predicament. After looking for almost half an hour for the cows, Gail and I realized that they must have gone into the deep, mysterious woods at the back of the pasture. Fear accompanied us as we treaded gingerly into the woods, as we had been warned that quicksand and bears existed in the forest. At the same time, thunder started booming loudly, and lightning furiously erupted in the dark sky. We didn't get very far into the thick woods before looking at each other and turning around. We quickly ran back into the pasture. By this time, it was raining hard. Without too much hesitation, we agreed to go home without the cows. Knowing that we would be in trouble and afraid of the storm, we were both starting to cry by this time. At one point, ignorant of the lightning risks, we tried to take refuge under a tree, but that didn't provide any shelter, so we quickly moved toward home.

When Gail and I got back to the house, we were soaked and dirty from sliding down the slope near the creek. My dad was home from work already, sitting at the kitchen table. He was very unhappy that we had failed in bringing home the cows. I am sure that he was also very tired after working his day job as a mechanic at the local iron ore mine. I could see disappointment and growing anger in his eyes. He didn't scream as my mother did, but his temper was very unpleasant. He would roll his eyes, grit his teeth and mutter something unintelligible as if he was trying to minimize his anger. I felt ridiculed by the eye-rolling and condemned by the angry emanations billowing from him. I would try not to cry because it would only increase the intensity of my father's anger.

I would later feel angry at how unfair my father was. I felt worthless, wondering why I was so unlovable that even my own father didn't care about me. It seemed that we children were only valuable to my parents for the work that we accomplished for them. I thought that if my father actually loved us, he would have shown at least a little concern for our well-being. Instead of concern for us, he was only angry that we didn't bring the cows home for milking.

Eventually, my soul became damaged by the growing anxiety in me. My nightmares became more frequent. I became more introverted and mistrustful of others. Mainly, I tried very hard to avoid causing anger in my parents.

Trauma on a Horse

Summer of 1962, Northern Minnesota Dairy Farm

One summer day after fourth grade in 1962, when I was nine years old, I became the main cow herder at our small dairy farm. Instead of bringing the cows home on foot, I would now be rounding up the cows on a horse. I was excited yet scared about my new chore. Our family had gotten a good, easy-to-handle horse a couple of years earlier. My oldest sister, who was six years older than I, had been riding him before I learned to ride.

The horse was a nine-year-old Pinto named Pat. I had been riding for about a year now, but I had just learned how to put the saddle on Pat by myself. I wasn't very skilled at the task. Being unsupervised, I was a little nervous, but the chore needed to be done, so I went to the barn to retrieve the saddle.

I weighed about sixty-five pounds, so grabbing the heavy, forty-pound, Western saddle from the barn and dragging it to where the horse was standing was a large task in itself. With all my might, I threw it up on the horse's back. Grabbing the strap hanging down on the other side of Pat's belly, I tried to tighten the saddle on his back.

Pat knew just what to do to make it more difficult for me. Holding his breath after inhaling, he extended his belly just as I was cinching up the saddle. Ignorant of the fact that the saddle was not snuggly secure, I went through the motions of mounting the horse. Pushing up my white glasses and taking a deep breath of the cool, piney, northern Minnesota air, I grabbed the reins, put my left foot in the stirrup, and pulled myself up onto the saddle.

After I got on the horse, I lightly nudged him with my heels and steered him with the reins toward the smaller field on our farm to find the cows. After trotting down a narrow path through the forest for about a quarter of a mile, we arrived at our destination. As we came into the clearing, I saw the cows grazing on the far side of the pasture.

I was about to steer Pat toward the cows when he suddenly reared up. Simultaneously, I gasped as I saw a black bear charging out of the left side of the thick woods toward us. I suddenly realized that we might have gotten between her and her cubs. In the shock of the commotion, I dropped the reins as the horse bolted away from the bear toward the right side of the woods. Since I couldn't stop him without the control of the reins, I hastily grabbed the saddle horn, threw my legs behind me, and lowered my head. My only thought at that moment was to stay on the horse. The forest was very thick, full of many different-sized pine and birch trees, and filled in with brush. I knew that I would get ripped off the horse or worse if I didn't get my legs out of the stirrups and keep my head down.

Even though adrenaline was pumping furiously through my veins, I tried to keep calm. The small woods led down a hill toward the small, round lake in the middle of our property. I expected a sharp turn soon, knowing that if the horse didn't make a quick turn at the bottom of the hill, he would end up in the lake. Sure enough, Pat made a sharp right turn, still galloping hard. The centrifugal force from the turn caused the saddle and I to flip under the horse. Panic engulfed me as I felt myself roll with the saddle under the horse. Gravity then took effect, and I hit the ground. I immediately saw Pat's hind-leg hooves in the air coming towards my head. Instinctively, I closed my eyes, waiting for my head to be crushed. Unbelievably, the horse missed my head.

As I lay on the ground, Pat kept galloping toward home. With the saddle's stirrups comically flailing under his belly, he ran until he was out of sight. I shakenly stood up. At first, shock from the jarring incident kept me from feeling any physical pain, so I just stood there numbly for a minute or two.

After the initial shock wore away, I realized that my glasses were not on my face. I frantically wondered, "Where are they?" I got back down on my knees and feverishly began looking for them. I finally found them in tall grass not far from where I fell off of the horse. I stood up after I picked them up. At first, I just blankly stared at the crushed glasses. After a few seconds, I began to wonder what punishment awaited me. With the pieces of my broken glasses in my small hands, trauma from the incident vibrating in my soul, and fearful thoughts echoing in my mind, I began to sob as I walked home.

My dad was not my first concern after the incident because he would not be directly involved with the consequences of my destroyed glasses. It was my mother who would be inconvenienced when she took me to the eye doctor. She was the one who controlled the purse strings, and she did not like spending money or time on her children. She would not be happy about the added expense for new eyeglasses. I only went to the doctor if it was absolutely necessary. As a young child, I suffered through many ear infections and even a carbuncle of boils without a trip to the doctor.

As I expected, when I got to the house, I never had a chance to tell my mom about what had happened. She saw the broken glasses in my hands and became angry. She stared menacingly at me for a second before starting to scream at me. Since I was already traumatized, I blocked out what she was yelling. I just stood there and absorbed her anger. As she continued to scream at me, condemnation invaded my soul, even though I knew that I couldn't have stopped the event from happening. Because my life was controlled by a tyrannical spirit, I didn't dare to stand up for myself. I had no recourse but to feel traumatized, condemned, and devalued.

The next week, when my mom took me to the eye doctor to get another prescription, I received amazing news. I didn't need to wear glasses anymore. I had been wearing them since the first grade to correct a lazy eye. For a few months, I even had to wear a black patch over one eye in order to force the lazy eye to work harder. Wearing a black patch on my white glasses while modeling my dad's bowl-like haircut incurred merciless teasing at school. However, since I was faithful to wear my glasses, the method had worked. I was so happy that I didn't need the glasses anymore, and my mom was relieved that she didn't have to buy me another pair.

Author at age 9

Because of my parent's arbitrary childrearing methods, I didn't always know when my parents would be really angry with me. This time, I wasn't punished further for my broken glasses. The added punishment might have been a spanking from my dad. If we defied him, though, he could be even harsher.

My dad wanted to be a good father, so I don't think he meant to hurt us, but he was impatient and had a temper when I was young. He may have been suffering from Post-Traumatic Stress Disorder from his experiences in the army while stationed in the Philippines during World War II. He may have felt enormous stress from working a full-time job and running a farm at the same time to support his large family. I did forgive him for his harshness later in life after I realized that it is impossible to be a perfect parent in this imperfect world.

Without understanding the reasons for my father's anger as a child, I could only be afraid of him. Sometimes, like in my earlier memory, I was very afraid of him.

An Angry Beating

One evening in 1962, when I was nine and supposedly asleep in my bedroom, I heard a loud commotion coming from the living room. I snuck out of my room and went into the hallway to see what was happening. As I peered around the corner into the living room, I saw my father violently kicking one of my older sisters as she lay on the living room floor.

When my father spanked us, it was painful both physically and emotionally. He was usually angry when he did it. This punishment was different. It was much more severe. As I fearfully cringed against the hallway wall, I watched the rest of the event unfold.

My sister must have defied my father in some way. I wasn't sure if she was unconscious, but when my father was done kicking her, she was silent. My mother was standing close by but did not intervene during the ordeal. As my sister lay unmoving on the floor, my dad stormed out of the house. I stood fearfully in the hallway for a few more seconds. Then, I slipped back into my bedroom, feeling helpless and cowardly for not running to see if my sister was okay. Because I was afraid that I would be in trouble if I had been seen, I quietly crawled back into bed. I never heard anything more about the incident or why it happened that night. I never asked anyone about it either. Fear and intimidation kept me quiet.

The many bad interactions that I experienced and witnessed in my childhood impressed on me that I was not important. Even though my parents tried to raise their children right, the spirit of tyranny had invaded their parenting. Even though they were known as good people in the community and attended church faithfully, their parenting methods were devoid of love and nurturing. Instead of finding and developing my strengths and abilities, I focused mainly on avoiding punishment. While feeling helpless, I was taught to be anxious, fearful, and distrustful, which in turn stunted the growth of my abilities and my personality.

Moving to the Big Farm

Summer of 1964, Northern Minnesota Family Farm

In 1964, when I was eleven, we moved from the small milking farm to the big agricultural farm, previously owned by my great-grandparents prior to their deaths. My dad had inherited some money during that same year, so he had enough to purchase the farm. The farm had some livestock, including a couple of horses and a couple of beef cattle. Potatoes, hay, and oats were now the main agricultural products. We also had a small tree farm, growing mostly Christmas trees and some decorative shrubs.

The farmhouse had been built by my great-grandparents in the early 1900s. It was a well-built, five-bedroom, two-story house. It had beautiful wooden floors throughout the house. There was a lovely, plant-filled sunroom, separated from the living room by elegant French doors. The house overlooked a large potato field, which was majestically lined by tall Norway pines. A large, gray, wooden warehouse for storing potatoes existed behind the house. Right next to the warehouse, a big white barn stood. It was used mainly for storing hay in the winter. Feral cats would also have their kittens there. Right next to the barn sat a small silo for storing oats, which would feed the horses in the winter.

I spent most of my time at home either in or around the barn caring for the livestock or in the warehouse grading potatoes with my father and siblings. Grading potatoes involved sorting through a mound of potatoes on a wooden grading platform. My dad would shovel the potatoes from the floor of the warehouse onto the platform. Then, we separated out the good potatoes from the rotting or green potatoes. We also saved some of the small or irregular potatoes for seed for next year's planting. Afterward, we would bag the good potatoes into ten and twenty-pound bags and load them into our white, one-ton van to deliver to the local grocery stores. We also sold them wholesale in fifty-pound burlap bags to people who would stop by the farm to buy them in bulk for a lower price.

During the first full summer at the big farm in 1965, my mom decided to oversee a major cleaning effort. One of the chores was to clean the outside windows. There were many windows to wash, including all of the sunroom windows and the large picture window in the dining room.

As I was handwashing dishes on one of those cleaning afternoons, my younger sister, Gail, was outside washing the kitchen window right in front of me. A storm was quickly approaching. The large pine trees in the front yard were starting to sway as the wind picked up. Lightning streaked across the sky as the booms of thunder got louder. Gail was standing high up on a ladder, crying as she went through the motions of washing the window. She repetitively lifted the rag from the wash bucket, which was sitting next to her on the ladder, up to the window. I felt sorry for her because at least I could stay dry and safe inside doing the dishes.

Gail was naturally afraid of the lightning from the approaching storm. She would look up at the sky, back at me, and then, still crying, keep washing the window. She had earlier asked if she could come into the house, but my mom wouldn't let her come in until she was done washing the window. It was painful to watch her emotionally suffer as the lightning got closer and rain started to fall. I was scared for her, but I was powerless to tell her to come inside. My mother seemed oblivious to my sister's dangerous and scary predicament. It appeared to me that the goal of getting the window washed was much more important to my mom than my sister's physical or emotional well-being.

After Gail finished the window, she finally came inside. She was okay physically, but she was an emotional mess, seemingly soaking wet from the crying as she was from the rain.

Macro and Micro Versions of Tyranny

Later in my life, I would think about how my soul, my hopes, and my abilities were almost destroyed by the tyranny in my growing-up years. I began to relate it to communist ideology and rule. I had studied Macro Economics, a branch of economics that deals with the structure and behavior of the whole economy, and Micro Economics, a branch of economics that studies the behavior of individuals and firms within the economy. I began to compare my life, the micro version of tyranny, to the experiences of the Czechoslovakian people, the macro version of tyranny.

Communist rule became tyrannical because it had to use force to control the people. The government forced individuals into assigned roles within a pre-planned economy. Meanwhile, it stripped individuals and businesses of the ownership of property, investment power, and their dreams for the future.

The people were given a similar wage based on the amount produced within the economy. This was done to ensure that the amount consumed would not be greater than the amount produced. Any dissenters were sent to jails. Some were sent to forced labor camps. Others were murdered. Government under communism became a cruel master, and the people became their slaves. It created mainly two classes of people, the communist rulers and the rest of the population. Gypsies, a very small minority group, were ignored and tolerated by the other two classes of people. The communist elite lived very well and kept themselves separate from the other people. Like in the novel *Animal Farm* by George Orwell, that elite thought that they were *more equal than the others.*

The lack of concern for the people by the elite communists reminded me of my childhood. Jobs were assigned to build wealth, mostly for the elite. I saw similarities in how the elite treated the workers in Czechoslovakia and how my parents treated their children working on the farm that they owned. My mother would make cookies for my dad's daily consumption, but she forbade me from having any of them. While the elites lived well, the workers only had their basic needs met.

The best years of my young life were during my years of high school because I spent much more time away from home. The effects of tyranny followed me, though. I still struggled with anxious feelings of doubt and low self-esteem, and I had a lack of trust in others. I tried to keep these true thoughts and feelings to myself as a protection against the disdain of others and from a fear of punishment from my parents. I didn't even let my friends know about the insecurities lurking inside me.

Amazingly, I saw signs that some Czechoslovakians had the same issue. Many were afraid to tell me their story for fear of retribution. If they did tell me something, they did not want me to record their names; hence, I do not have names to share with their stories. People did not look me in the eye when I spoke with them. I saw fear in them, and I realized that I had suffered from a similar paralyzing fear in my life. As a young woman, I could not easily look people in the eye.

Although I believe that the threat of death or prison was the main reason for fear in the Czechoslovakians, I know that some had experienced rape. I had been told by a number of people that I met in Czechoslovakia that both the Nazis and the communists had committed rape. It was used by the communist enforcers to subdue the people after World War II. Oppressors do not value other people. They will use any tool available to obtain and keep themselves in power, and rape is one of those instruments in tyranny's toolbox.

Rape is personal and effective in squelching independence. Ruthless power over another is its objective. Rape degrades the most intimate act that can happen between two people. What was designed to consummate a beautiful and loving relationship instead becomes a hideous act. Rape steals the souls of the people being raped. It creates havoc in society by destroying cohesiveness in families, the building blocks of society. It replaces self-confidence and trust with insecurity, mistrust, and shame. I know because I also experienced rape as a teenager. The rape was the beginning of my spiral into hopelessness. I would experience years of suffering before being enlightened and starting my life anew.

Entering Prague

June 1990, Prague, Czechoslovakia

In June of 1990, after experiencing many years of suffering under tyranny, the people of Prague were also starting anew. Prague is the historical capital city of Czechoslovakia. Currently, it is the capital of the Czech Republic since Slovakia split from Czechoslovakia in January of 1993.[26] It is a very old, major European city. After the Iron Curtain fell in 1989, it again became a major international city.

As our tour bus first drove into the city of Prague, I found myself dumbfoundedly staring at the earth-toned buildings passing by as our bus drove down narrow cobblestone streets. Like in the village of Chynice, there was very little color in the city. I could still see dignity in the ancient structures as they were solidly built. As we approached the center of the city, I saw the famous Charles Bridge, which connects the city to the majestic castle complex on the other side of the river. It took my breath away as I realized that I was seeing a historical city that most of the West hadn't seen in over forty years.

---

26 Wikipedia, 2021

Like Vienna, Prague is full of history. I was most intrigued with the old, mysterious Charles Bridge. It is lined on both sides of its walkway with the statues of about thirty Christian saints. The bridge crosses the Vltava River, which runs through the center of Prague. Its construction started in 1357 during the reign of King Charles IV and was completed in the beginning of the fifteenth century.[27] The bridge is the most important connection between Prague Castle and the city's Old Town. Historically, it linked the trade route between Eastern and Western Europe. When I first viewed the bridge, I imagined a kingly procession of knights on horses with kings and queens in carriages crossing the bridge on the way to the medieval castle.

After checking into our hotel, I couldn't wait to go exploring. I had made an arrangement with my tour guide to separate from the tour group to do my own research for my independent study. It was very exciting but a little scary to be on my own. On that first afternoon in Prague, though, the warm, sunny day was calling to me to start my walk towards Charles Bridge.

As I started walking, the birds in the nearby trees seemed to be very loudly chirping in contrast to the quietness of the cobblestone streets. The city streets

27   Id.

were almost deserted, but after a couple of blocks of walking, I ran into a small celebration at a pub. I stopped in the entryway and observed a group of older men quietly talking and laughing while drinking their beer. They seemed to be cautiously but joyously celebrating their new freedom.

I also saw a group of soldiers standing on the street close to the pub. Communist troops still kept order in the city, but in my ignorance of the danger that they posed, I did not feel too intimidated by them. As I kept on walking, I felt bewildered by the lack of people and commerce along the way.

After a few more minutes of walking, the Charles Bridge came into view. I couldn't wait to explore it. At the same time, I glanced across the river and saw very large steeples and towers jutting out from the Prague Castle wall. They looked dark, majestic, and ominous as they towered above the castle like skyscrapers tower over a modern city from afar.

As I approached the bridge, I smelled acrid air coming from the polluted river. My sense of smell soon dimmed when I stopped in awe as I saw up-close the ancient, dignified-looking statues aligned on both sides of the bridge. The statues were darkened with age, but the intricate details of the carvings were still visibly impressive. Overwhelmed with curiosity about the statues, I began to walk across the bridge. The bridge is a third of a mile long and was empty of pedestrian traffic, so I didn't feel rushed and took my time taking in the sights. I was still amazed at the quietness of the city. Very little foot, car, or boat traffic existed.

I tried to read the writings on the first statues that were posed along both sides of the bridge. Unable to read any meaning from the inscriptions, I was able to at least decipher a few of the names on the statues. I wasn't familiar with some of them. The names included John of Matha, Felix of Valois, Norbert of Xanten, Wenceslas, Sigismund, the Madonna, and Thomas Aquinas.

Charles Bridge Saint Norbert of Xanten, Wenceslas and Sigismund

After crossing the bridge, I climbed the incline of a small street leading to the Prague castle wall. The castle sits high on a hill overlooking the Charles Bridge and is the largest ancient castle in the world. After a few more minutes of strenuous walking up the New Castle Stairs, I reached the entrance to the castle at Hradcany Square. The square was mainly deserted, so I quickly continued to the front of the gate. Since there were no crowds, I was able to immediately enter the castle.

I walked through the first and second courtyards of the castle, stopping after I passed through a hallway and entered the third courtyard. Right in front of me was St. Vitus Cathedral. The cathedral was massive. I looked up at all the intricate details of the church in astonishment. There are two portals, the St. Wenceslas portal and the St. Adalber portal. Above them are two gothic towers, each being about two hundred and sixty feet high. Above the portals is the main attraction, the Rose. The Rose is a huge, circular-looking stained-glass window featuring the creation as told in the Bible. It is an intricate mosaic of colored glass. I stood in awe as my eyes traveled upward to take in the view. It took my breath away.

Another entryway is called the Golden Gate and is located on the south side of the cathedral. Above the entrance is mosaic creation of thirty-one shades of colored glass that depicts the Last Judgment. It was completed in 1371 under Charles IV, the king of Bohemia and the Holy Roman Emperor. The mosaic covers 904 square feet. In it, the figure of Christ is surrounded by angels in the center, and beneath it are the figures of six Czech saints. The entire background of the mosaic was originally in gold, so it was named The Golden Gate.[28]

South Side of St. Vitus Cathedral

---

28 The Getty Conservation Institute, December 1998

After I had spent enough time looking at the almost scary, gothic exterior of the huge cathedral, I decided to explore the grounds further before going inside. As I walked around, I saw a few palaces, although they looked more like old mansions to me. They looked like five-story, large, square houses built adjacent to one another along the brick and stone streets. I also walked by St. George's Basilica, which was built in the year 920.[29] It is the oldest surviving church in the palace area, but it is much smaller than the cathedral.

Eventually, I meandered down an old cobblestone street lined with a number of very old shops, which were not open at the time. They looked like relics from the Middle Ages. The shops were not very large, and the doors to them were not very tall. I was fascinated by the sights, but since nothing was open, I decided to turn around and walk back to the area around the cathedral.

After a few minutes of walking, I found myself in front of the Old Royal Palace. The gothic structure of the palace dates back to the ninth century, but the current building can only be traced back to the fourteenth century and Emperor Charles IV, the father of

29 Wikipedia, 2021

King Wenceslas.[30] Within the palace is a structure that I did not get to see, called Viadislav Hall. It was built much later than the palace in the sixteenth century. Initially, the hall was used for coronations, banquets, markets, and even jousting tournaments. Today, it is used for state functions.

I soon found the main entrance to the Old Royal Palace but was abruptly stopped by a soldier acting as a security guard. He stared at me menacingly. I felt very intimidated and quickly turned around to leave the palace. I had wondered why I was unable to enter at the time, but I was told later that government meetings were taking place in the palace. Since security was very tight, I was not allowed to enter. I also learned later that Shirley Temple was the new U.S. Ambassador to Czechoslovakia and was somewhere in the castle, but I would not get the chance to meet her.

After being denied entrance to the palace, I walked back to St. Vitus Cathedral. St. Vitus was a Sicilian martyr and the patron saint of Bohemia, actors, and dancers.[31] The cathedral is a gothic masterpiece. It has many ancient-looking adornments and gargoyles displayed all over its exterior. The spires right above the

---

30 Prague Castle for Visitors, 2021
31 Wikipedia, 2021

church entrance look as if they are guarding the very old, large, heavy entrance doors.

I finally entered the cathedral. As my eyes focused, I was overtaken by the sprawling beauty of its intricate architecture. The ceiling towered majestically above me. A wave of vertigo hit me as I looked up at the colorful and exquisite stained-glass windows. After steadying myself, I continued to walk through the cathedral.

Inside St. Vitus Cathedral

Much like the cathedral in Vienna, the interior is also full of beautiful statues and altars. It also contains the tombs of many Bohemian kings and Holy Roman Emperors. Saint Wenceslas, who was the Duke of Bohemia from 921 to 935, is commemorated here.[32] The Christmas carol, *Good King Wenceslas*, was written to honor him as he was beloved by the people that he ruled. There is also a statue of him on a horse in Wenceslas Square, the main city square in Prague. Wenceslas Square is located on the other side of the river from the castle.

St. Vitus Cathedral is the seat of the Catholic Archbishop of Prague. The building of the cathedral began in 1344, but due to wars and plagues, it wasn't finished until 1869.[33] The architecture is mostly of gothic style, but it has some Baroque and Renaissance inflections. The many stunning stained-glass windows towering above each room or chapel depict a number of different Christian saints and themes, including the Holy Trinity and The Last Judgment.

The Bohemian crown jewels, including the gold crown of St. Wenceslas, are also stored at the cathedral in Wenceslas Chapel. The crown contains some of

32 Wikipedia, 2021
33 Id.

the largest sapphires in the world. Although I didn't see the crown jewels, I did see many tombs, jeweled and golden altars, many artifacts, and numerous paintings from the fourteenth to the sixteenth centuries.

It took me a couple of hours to walk through most of the cathedral, although to truly appreciate the experience, I could have stayed all day. Unfortunately, my eyes had become totally saturated by all of the overwhelming sights. The day was growing shorter, and I was ready to leave and get something to eat.

After I left the cathedral, I took in the view of the Charles Bridge from the castle entrance. It was stunning. I could almost see the whole city from this vantage point. While I was taking in the view, I saw a street artist painting the same scene, so I bought a painting from him. I also bought a painting when I went back to the city in 2019 from another street artist. The difference between 1990 and 2019 was huge. In 1990, I only saw one artist situated at the castle overlooking the bridge, and he used only pencil and watercolors to paint his pictures. In 2019, there were multiple artists and many other vendors. In 1990, the area was completely void of commerce, compared to the bustling scene that I saw in 2019.

Street Artist on Prague Castle wall

First Night in Prague

In June of 1990, and unbeknownst to me, a curfew was still being imposed on the population of Prague. Because of my ignorance as to why the streets were becoming totally deserted, I stopped at a restaurant just before dark on my first evening in Prague.

As I peeked into the restaurant, an engaging, middle-aged waiter waved me inside. The man was also the manager of the restaurant. He was almost bald and stood at about five feet, six inches, making him only a couple of inches taller than I. His graying eyebrows would slightly lift every time he smiled.

The restaurant had about seven empty tables. I chose a table next to a window facing the street. As I sat down, the waiter brought me a menu, but since it wasn't in English, I could only laugh and shrug my shoulders. An aroma of fresh bread swirled around in the restaurant and fueled my hunger. Not soon enough, he brought back a plate of delicious beef stew and a couple of freshly made rolls. I hadn't eaten since morning, so I tried not to wolf down the food too quickly.

Using a made-up sign language, we had an amusing conversation of misunderstandings while I ate my dinner. When I was almost finished, he sat down next to me and pointed through the window at some soldiers marching by. I didn't quite understand what he was trying to tell me, but I did sense that he was trying to hurry me through my dinner. Although I am sure that he wanted to close the restaurant for the evening, he also seemed very concerned about me. I quickly finished my dinner and paid the bill. As I was about to walk out the door, the waiter kindly gave me a small porcelain creamer decanter as a souvenir. Then, he hurried me out of the restaurant.

As I walked down the street, I noticed the same soldiers marching down the street only a block away. I felt some fear and picked up my walking speed, but I didn't realize that I could have been arrested for breaking curfew since it was dark by the time I got back to the hotel.

As I got ready for bed that night, I reviewed the day's experiences. I had witnessed some people in Prague cautiously beginning their new lives, but I also realized that something new was happening inside of me. I had come a long way from Minnesota to this strange and wonderful city of Prague, but my inner voyage had also traveled miles away from the scared young woman I had been when I got married.

My Wedding

February 1974, Hometown in Northern Minnesota

My husband and I were married in early February of 1974. It was a sad day. His church did not approve of our marriage, mainly because he was Protestant and I was raised as a Catholic. I was also a sinner who had gotten pregnant outside of marriage. Both of us were young and not ready to make a lifetime commitment. I thought that we loved each other at the time, but since my upbringing wasn't loving and secure, I really didn't know much about love.

My husband and I had known each other since high school, but we didn't start dating until our first semester in college in the fall of 1971. I knew that our churches were not compatible, so I started attending a Baptist church with him when we became more serious with each other in 1973.

I didn't spend a lot of time with his family, so I didn't know how much they disapproved of me. I am not sure that they even knew much about our relationship because when we went home from college for a weekend or for holidays, we did not visit each other's homes. We also spent the summers apart. I realize that not spending time with his parents should have alerted me to potential problems in our relationship, but I was very unwise. I had been afraid of most men after the rape that I experienced when I was a teenager, but I felt comfortable with my soon-to-be husband. I knew him, and I believed that he was a good man. I also believed that he cared about me since he had been the one who initially pursued me.

I didn't realize that I would not be fully accepted into his family until I found out that I was pregnant. My in-laws were very unhappy when we announced our engagement. I sat through a long lecture about how I was ruining their son's life. My parents were also very unhappy with me. I felt totally blamed for becoming pregnant.

My husband-to-be must have aligned himself with the disapprovers because, at our wedding, he seemed angry with me. Even though he knew that we had been taking a risk prior to my becoming pregnant, he appeared to totally blame me. However, it was a common practice in 1974 for women to bear the shame for an out-of-wedlock pregnancy, so it wasn't surprising that I shouldered all of the blame.

In spite of the disapproval from both of our parents and our community, we got married a month later. The wedding was held at my hometown Catholic church. After the wedding, my parents and his parents had separate gatherings at their respective homes.

No polite conversations occurred between his parents and my parents at the dinner that was held in the basement of the Catholic church after the ceremony. There was one brief exchange between my husband's dad and my mom. We had ordered a bottle of champagne to be served at the head table for the wedding toasts. My husband's parents didn't drink, except for medicinal purposes. Before the toasts began, my new father-in-law turned to my mother and gave her his small glass. I sensed that he was virtue signaling by saying, "You would probably enjoy this more than I." My mother became incensed and retorted, "You are a very rude man."

After the wedding dinner, we stopped first at my parent's house. Everyone was having a festive time. We walked into the house without much fanfare. Because of the dysfunction in my family, I felt uncomfortable and almost invisible. Sensing that my husband was also uncomfortable around my family, I quickly went upstairs to my old bedroom, changed, and packed up my things. Looking around my room, I realized that I would never again call this my home. Remembering my earlier hope for a happy family, I felt a deep sadness come over me. With a sense of impending doom, I went back downstairs, and without much of a send-off, we left the house and got into our car to go to my new in-law's house.

It was a smaller gathering at my husband's home and much less festive. As we went into the house, I saw a handful of people sitting at the dining room table in front of a large picture window.

My husband's parents had a nice lake home. It was a log cabin with a newer addition that had modernized it into a very comfortable home. The snowy lake was visible through the glistening birch and pine trees growing between the dock and the picture window. A bird feeder was hung from one of the tall pine trees just outside the window. It attracted many birds and provided entertainment for everyone seated in front of it at the dining room table. My new mother-in-law was in her cozy kitchen, getting ready to serve coffee and apple pie.

As we entered the house, my husband greeted his parents and their friends, whom I am sure had come over to commiserate with them about the wedding. I stood behind my husband. As I stood there, I realized that I was making everyone feel uncomfortable, so I went to sit in the living room by myself.

I sensed that I was wearing the scarlet letter of shame. I wanted to run away, but I had nowhere to go. I wanted to leave as quickly as we left my parent's house, but my husband didn't seem to want to leave. For about another hour, I ruefully sat in the living room wondering if I had made a huge mistake by getting married while my husband enjoyed his conversation with his parents and their friends. When it finally started to get dark, late into the afternoon, he finally got up from the table to say goodbye. I got up to follow him.

As we walked outside, there was an unhappy silence between us. We gingerly walked down the icy sidewalk, quietly shivering as we approached our car. I noticed that no one had applied *Just Married* decorations. It was fitting. Our wedding was uncelebrated and uncongratulated. It was also very appropriate that it was now dark and extremely cold outside. It mirrored my feelings about the day.

Later, when I looked at some of our wedding pictures, I noticed that neither my husband nor I are smiling much. It was a horribly cold day, and not just because of the below-zero weather. Joy was totally missing at the wedding. The whole day felt more like a funeral. It was an event that would inflame gossip in my hometown. Just a couple of years before, I had good standing in my community, receiving scholarships and awards. Now, my reputation was completely destroyed.

My husband had not reserved a hotel room for our wedding night, so we drove south to Duluth, Minnesota, and stopped at the first hotel with a vacancy. Ironically, the only available room was a honeymoon suite. It was more expensive than we could really afford. Another wasted expense was the purchase of a negligee for the occasion. We didn't say much to each other. It was late, so we just went to sleep. We had to be up early to drive back to Minneapolis for my husband's job as a singer at a downtown Baptist church.

After the wedding, romance and happiness eluded us. We didn't discuss our dreams and plans for the future. I wanted to have a happy family, which I thought everyone wanted. I am guessing that my husband's main dream was to become a famous singer. He didn't seem ready to be a husband or a father. We were unlikely to accomplish either of our dreams together. Our life together began like two unhappy mules yoked together but wanting to go different ways. Without the blessing of our families, our marriage was already doomed for failure. The spirit of tyranny had doubled down on its power over my life. I became more depressed and felt a greater sense of worthlessness.

The Birth of My Son

August 1974, Minneapolis, Minnesota

After our wedding in February of 1974, my husband and I moved into a small one-bedroom apartment in South Minneapolis, not far from the downtown area. I had quit college and gotten a job as a typist at a major insurance company. I would ride the bus on Hennepin Avenue to and from work. My husband drove to and from the University of Minnesota for classes. He was studying music as a voice major.

I tried very hard to make us a home while supporting us with my income. My husband worked on getting his college degree. I tried to be a good wife and did all of the household chores. I was also looking forward to being a mom. Even so, our marriage was not much of a marriage. It felt like I was living with a roommate that I didn't know well rather than a husband. We rarely talked to each other, even when we spent time together.

When the summer came, my pregnancy was starting to really show. Still taking the bus to work, I would sometimes run into issues. I never thought much about sexism at the time. I just wanted to have a happy family. I was willing to work up until I had the baby to help support us, but my motives for working during my pregnancy were misunderstood by some.

I would often get odd looks in downtown Minneapolis because of my condition. I think some were looks of concern, but other looks seemed condemning. One day, when the bus was very full, I boarded it to head home after work. As I stood, holding on to the metal pole to keep my balance as the bus took off, a man sitting next to me loudly scoffed, "I am not giving up my seat for a woman's libber." I didn't react or say anything back to him. Even though I didn't show any emotion, the pain went deep as I accepted the condemnation. I was also very embarrassed by the negative attention. No one else on the bus said anything. Some had at first stared at me but then uncomfortably looked away.

I was becoming used to being judged harshly by others. It seemed to me that almost everyone in my life was ashamed of me. When my coworkers found out that I had gotten pregnant before my marriage, I was ostracized. I felt very alone, worthless, and very unlovable.

On August 17, 1974, my water broke while I was in my apartment kitchen. I was a week overdue and very uncomfortable by this time. Anxiously awaiting the moment, I was also scared. It was a Saturday morning, so my husband was home with me. After I grabbed my small suitcase, he drove me to the hospital.

When we arrived at the hospital, I was quickly admitted since I was already in labor. My son, Brian, was born about eight hours later. The labor was more painful than I had imagined. I needed many stitches afterward, but the worst of the experience was that I was alone and very scared after my baby boy was born.

Brian didn't cry. Without saying anything to me, the doctors quickly took him out of the labor room. My husband wasn't with me throughout my labor and delivery, so I had no one to support me or ask questions for me. I had no family members close by to turn to for support, but I wouldn't have asked them for help anyway. After my baby was whisked away, I was left alone with my thoughts and fears. I had a fitful night's sleep.

The next morning, a nurse stopped by to see me. She looked at me without much warmth and asked me, "Do you know about your baby's condition?"

Since I still had not seen a doctor or Brian yet, I was very distraught inside but fearful of showing emotion to such a cold stranger. I stared back at her, but I didn't utter a sound. She then stated, "Your baby had a seizure right after he was born, and he is in observation. A doctor will stop by later to explain everything to you and answer any questions." She abruptly turned around and left me alone in my room. Feeling very upset, I also had many unanswered questions.

Later in the day, the doctor stopped by. He said, "Your baby did not get enough oxygen during birth and had a seizure right after he was born. We will keep him in observation for a couple of more days, and if he doesn't have another seizure, we will let you both go home."

Soon after the doctor left my room, I was allowed to go and see Brian. I wanted to hold him, but I was not yet able to do so since he was on an IV and still being watched carefully. Soon, I waddled back to my hospital room, feeling sore, scared, and alone. That night, during visiting hours, my husband came to see me, bringing one of my best friends from college. It was good to see her, but I sensed aloofness in my husband. I am sure that he went to see Brian, but we didn't talk about it. We did not even discuss the events of Brian's birth. My visitors left after a couple of hours, and I was alone again for the night.

On the third day, Brian and I went home. The doctor had put him on phenobarbital, a narcotic sedative, to prevent him from having any more seizures. He slept a lot. I didn't learn until after I had my second child that babies are usually awake more often. He was on the medication for a year and never had another seizure.

Brian was almost bald, with only blond fringes at the base of his head. He had handsome, symmetrical features and weighed eight pounds, ten ounces. I couldn't have been happier to be a new mom. For the first time in my life, I had someone to love.

Life on the Road

February 1975, Miami Beach, Florida

After Brian was born in August of 1974, my husband took a hiatus from college. We instead traveled with an off-Broadway show. It was good to get away from the bad start in our life together. My husband was one of a cast of six in the show performing the music of World War II.

Since I had nothing to do with the show, I felt invisible in this new life, but I didn't mind. I loved being a new mom. The cast members didn't mind having Brian along since he was such a cute and happy baby. I was given kudos for being a good mom. My husband got good marks for his wonderful tenor voice in the entertainment review section of the local papers. It was basically a good experience for all of us.

The show visited a number of cities, including Omaha, Indianapolis, Cincinnati, and Miami. The first time that I actually attended the show was at the Marco Polo Hotel in Miami Beach in February of 1975. The Marco Polo Hotel was a luxurious oceanfront hotel in the 1970s. It was the scene of high-class entertainment. Across the road from the hotel, Sammy Davis Jr. was performing at another venue. I was amazed and awed by the surroundings. It was quite a contrast to my life in cold, snowy Minneapolis.

My husband and I were staying at a complex of cottages just a couple of miles away from the hotel. Our cottage was a furnished one-bedroom unit with a small kitchen, a bathroom, and a tiny living room. It had vinal floors throughout. The only rug was near our bed in the bedroom.

On the first morning at the cottage, I was startled awake when I saw a large cockroach scoot across the floor of our bedroom. I had never seen such a large bug before in my life. I first screamed and then called the apartment manager. An exterminator came out right away.

The rest of the stay was pleasant. The Florida sunny skies, white sand beaches, and the palms swaying in the breeze were exotic and very inviting to me. I would take Brian for long walks in his stroller every day.

During the first couple of weeks, I had gotten to know an older lady who lived next door. She was kind and good with Brian. One day, she offered to watch Brian so that I could go with my husband to see the show. I felt a little nervous about leaving Brian, but I agreed.

It was a late afternoon on a Saturday in February of 1975. Getting ready for the evening, I put on a little make-up, combed my long, brown hair, and slid my five-foot, four-inch frame into my only floor-length, black dress. I was nervous because I did not know any of the cast members well yet. I would also be sitting alone in the dinner theatre for the whole evening. Even though I had been to a number of my husband's many performances by myself, including some operas, this would be a new experience for me.

When I was ready, my husband and I got into our car to go to the Marco Polo Hotel. After we arrived, we parked in the main parking lot close to the entrance of the hotel and exited the car. I soon noticed a middle-aged black man leave the hotel and walk toward us. As he approached, he started smiling. He stopped right in front of us, seeming to know my husband. I found out later that he was performing at another bar in the hotel. When he greeted us, my husband introduced me to him.

The man's name was Fats Domino. I was very surprised since I knew that he was a famous singer. He was especially well-known for his hit, *Blueberry Hill*. As I smiled, the singer took my hand and kissed it, saying, "You are a very beautiful woman." I blushed and stammered quietly, "Thank you." I felt very unsure of myself, as I had never been greeted in such a formal way before this time. I do not remember much about the rest of the evening, but I will always remember Mr. Domino's gentlemanly kindness toward me.

Overall, traveling with the show was a good experience, even though my own husband seemed like a stranger to me. As a performer, he had become a different personality from the one that I had known in college. He was much more confident around others and much more indifferent towards me. I felt almost nonexistent around him.

Except for being a mom, which was very important to me, the rest of my life was in limbo. I tried to avoid being a bother to the people in the show. With Brian in a stroller, I would instead occupy myself by exploring the local surroundings of each city that we visited. My husband immersed himself in his acting and singing role, enjoying the applause and the camaraderie of his fellow cast members. We did very little together as a family.

Suddenly, after traveling with the show for about a year, my husband made a decision to go back to school and finish his degree. We headed back to Minneapolis.

Back in Minneapolis

September 1975, Minneapolis, Minnesota

While my husband registered for classes in the fall of 1975, I got a night job at a major car rental company as a keypuncher. My husband had an opera workshop class that was scheduled for the late afternoon, so he could not make it back home until six o'clock in the evening. I was very upset that I had to find a babysitter. There was another woman in the apartment building who also had a baby, so I asked her if she would be willing to babysit Brian for a couple of hours until my husband got home from school. She declined. I had no relatives close by, so all I could do was look in the paper for someone to watch Brian. Soon, I interviewed and hired a lady from one of the ads in the paper.

The babysitter was a young woman, probably in her early thirties. She seemed nice, and Brian would be the only baby in her care. She lived alone in a small apartment building a couple of blocks away from mine. I had no reason to distrust her, but I was still very uncomfortable about leaving my baby with someone that I didn't know. She had no references, so I didn't know how trustworthy she was.

On the first night of my job, in the fall of 1975, I bundled up Brian, put him into the car, and drove to the babysitter's apartment. After parking and getting out of the car, I carried him into the building. My heart was sinking at the thought of leaving him with a stranger. When the lady took Brian out of my arms, he started to scream. As I turned around to leave, Brian was reaching out toward me and bawling his eyes out. He was only a year old. My heart broke, and tears rolled down my cheeks as I walked away. I had betrayed and abandoned my son. I felt like a terrible mother.

I didn't know if Brian would be mistreated or not, but at least I knew that he would only be there for a couple of hours. I thought that over time, he would adjust. However, he never did. Every time I dropped Brian off, he would scream and cry. I wanted to stay home with him, and I didn't want to have to leave him at this place. I was feeling angry that my husband didn't arrange his classes differently to work around my work schedule, but I didn't tell him how I felt. My husband and I were living in the same apartment, but we were not close as a young married couple should be. We did not share our inner concerns. I also didn't think that I had permission to complain about anything.

Life became routine in all other respects. My husband and I would not see much of each other. He would leave in the morning to go to school, then pick up Brian when he was done with his last class, feed him, and put him to bed at night. I would wake up with Brian the next morning, care for him all day, drop him off at the babysitter's house, and go to work. I left work at one o'clock in the morning, drove home, and went to bed by two o'clock. I was getting used to being lonely and not getting enough sleep.

I thought that I could manage the routine for a year while my husband finished college. But I never got used to dropping Brian off at the babysitter's house. One time when I dropped him off, a man with a dark, brooding look was sitting in her kitchen, and I was really scared for Brian. Because of the fear that I had of men and the fact that I had to work or we wouldn't have a place to live or food to eat, I was very conflicted. I wanted to take Brian home and tell my husband that we had to manage things differently. But I had no power within myself to do so. I was ruled by those tyrannical voices inside of me telling me that I had no other choice. I had to pay my penance for my sin. I had to work so that my husband could go to school, and therefore I had to have a babysitter.

After six months of working in data entry, I saw an ad on the bulletin board near the cafeteria for a new day position. I thought that it would be better for me to get a day job and find a decent daycare arrangement for Brian. My husband was still in college, and he had no plans yet of being able to help support us. I figured that if I could get the day job, I could at least make a little more money. I interviewed, took a test, and got the job. I was now a junior financial analyst.

Within another year, we moved into a different apartment in an old house near Minnehaha Park in south Minneapolis. My husband had quit school and found a job as an apprentice carpenter. It was hard for me to understand because he only had a couple of credits left to finish his degree. He seemed to be in a depression. Since we didn't discuss our feelings with each other, I am not sure what was truly going on inside of him. I was just glad that he was now making some money to help support us.

Before starting my new day job, I found a newly-established, institutionally-run daycare close by to my work. Again, my heart ripped open every time Brian cried and screamed as I dropped him off in the morning. I ruefully wondered, "How long can I go on feeling like a terrible mother?"

As the next few unhappy years went by, I evolved into a person without hope. I went through the motions of life, but I had no healthy connections to anyone. Brian had now become fearful, just like I had been as a child. I loved my son, but I felt powerless to help him. I couldn't even help myself.

Growing Tyranny in My Life

January 1981, Minneapolis, Minnesota

I turned twenty-eight years old in January of 1981. After being married to my husband for seven years, the culmination of the emotional pain from our unhappy marriage and the stress of working long hours without even small rewards for my hard work was taking effect. As Proverbs 13:12 states, "Hope deferred makes the heart sick." I was feeling hopeless living in a bad marriage and a loveless world. My heart was sick, and I wanted to die. I saw no way out of my trapped life. Like a bird in a cage, I felt exposed and unable to defend myself.

Many people wonder why a person stays in an unhappy marriage, and one answer, at least my answer, was that I did not have the means to leave. I had a child who needed my care. I had no means to accomplish all the things that needed to be done at the same time, such as work, retain a lawyer, and find a new place to live. We were barely keeping financially afloat with my job and my husband's job as a carpenter. The economy was sluggish in the late seventies and early eighties. Since the building trades are the first to be impacted in a recession, my husband did not have a steady paycheck. He spent most of his other time pursuing his musical theater ambitions, which did not pay much if anything. Most of all, I did not have the emotional strength to face the opposition that I sensed that I would have from my husband if I did leave him.

Even though my husband probably wanted me gone, he did not seem to want a divorce. Divorce was considered another major sin by both the Catholic and Protestant religions. I did not really want a divorce either, but I wanted a happy marriage, and that seemed out of reach.

I did not have family able or willing to help me either. My mother had told me once after I got married, "You have made your bed, and now you have to lay in it." The deep shame inside of me also kept me from communicating with anyone about my deep pain. I never considered seeing a counselor. Even if I had, I didn't have the money nor the time to spend on trying to sort out my life.

Eventually, the hurt in my life overwhelmed me. It felt like I was fighting an invincible barrier that stopped me from being successful at anything. It was also like I was on a sinister merry-go-round that kept going faster and faster. Hanging on to my sanity was like hanging on to that merry-go-round. As a result, keeping up with my schedule seemed harder and harder. Nothing that I did seemed to improve my life or my marriage. In fact, everything instead seemed to get worse. Eventually, I only saw darkness and failure. I tried to do everything right, but I felt unloved and disrespected, which only led to resentment and self-hatred.

It appeared to me that my husband pushed me away emotionally if I complained or tried to share any of my feelings. In the beginning of our marriage, I had accepted my plight. When it eventually became unbearable, I tried to talk to my husband about it. I just couldn't hold in my feelings anymore. As a result, after seven years of marriage, we did not have any positive interactions between us. I felt as if I had been sent to jail without any possibility of parole. I understand now that my husband was just as unhappy as I was and probably felt like he was in a prison, too. Hurting me was the outcome of his own hurt and disappointment.

Just like in my childhood, I was the source of exasperation for someone that I thought should love me.

The tyrannical spirit had complete control of me by now.

My Breakdown

In the early months of 1981, my days were filled with the routine of getting Brian off to school and then riding a bus from my house in south Minneapolis to the University of Minnesota. I had quit my job at the car rental company and gone back to school the year before. I wanted to finally finish my degree.

Since I was good at math, I decided that engineering was the path that I should take. Although not many women were in the engineering program, it was now not considered taboo. The woman's movement had made some progress in the ten years since I first started college in 1971. After being accepted into the university's electrical engineering program, I was now taking two classes a quarter. Also, I was working part-time at the University of Minnesota Medical School.

Even though I was passing my classes, I didn't feel like I was progressing fast enough. I felt old compared to the other students at the university, so I wanted to quickly finish my degree. The stress from the weight of my responsibilities and my unhappy marriage was beginning to overpower my strong will to succeed. My husband and I hardly even spoke to each other anymore. If we did, we would fight. It seemed like our fights were always right before a big test. I would then feel the stress from any ensuing argument on top of the stress of the big test.

I wasn't afraid of hard work, but my heart was sick. I had spent many nights over the past couple of years going from anger, sadness, and finally to despair. Sometimes I cried, and sometimes I yelled at God. I was struggling with a deep depression, and yet I had to keep going. The darkness in my soul kept growing. Previously, I wasn't a drinker, but I had begun drinking a glass or two of wine every night to help calm my nerves before going to sleep.

In my depression, I felt like I was in a deep, dark well. I couldn't climb out of the well. In my mind, no matter how hard I worked, success eluded me, and my personal life only got darker as time went on. I knew that I was not going to succeed. I believed that I had been dealt a bad hand, and nothing that I did would change my circumstances. The condemnation that I felt from my husband and his family, plus my own sin, weighed heavy on me. I could see my husband's sin as much as I could see mine, but I felt blamed for our bad marriage. The seedlings of self-hatred had grown into monstrous, painful thorns in my soul, and I was starting to think about suicide more and more.

At the time, my husband was singing as a tenor soloist at a large church in Minneapolis. The choir was about to take a trip to Florida with a production of the Messiah for Easter in the spring of 1981.

On the day that the choir left for Florida, I drove my husband to the church. After we arrived, he started to get out of the car. At the same time, a young woman ran out from the bus to meet him. She was short and blond and maybe a little younger than I. Without looking at me, my husband murmured a goodbye and got out of the car. Then, he opened the backseat door of the car and quickly grabbed his bag. As the young lady greeted him, he gave her the big smile that he used to give me. They both seemed like giddy teenagers excited for the trip. As I watched them board the bus together, heart-wrenching pain welled up in me. I went home feeling very alone and depressed.

That week, I went to stay with my husband's older brother and his wife at their home in Atlanta, Georgia. They had graciously bought me an airplane ticket. I stayed with them for a couple of days in their big, beautiful home until my husband came back from the performances in Florida. The choir was going to be stopping for another performance in Atlanta before heading back to Minnesota. Brian went to stay with my in-laws, so I knew that he was in good hands. My mother-in-law was a very kind person, although she was dismissive of me. Even so, I was glad that Brian adored his grandma, and his grandma adored him.

My sister-in-law was always very kind and accepting of me. She was tall, thin, and pretty, with lots of beautiful red hair. She was also very confident. Before becoming a lawyer, she had been a broadcaster at a local news channel in Minneapolis. My brother-in-law was a computer engineer. I never really got to know him. He tended to be quiet, keeping his opinions to himself.

I wondered if my sister-in-law understood my pain. She and my brother-in-law had moved away from Minnesota soon after they were married. I think that both of them understood that they needed space from the in-laws in order to cement their marriage connection. I felt closer to her than to the rest of my husband's family, even though we were not really close. Sometimes I felt inferior to her, but she always treated me with kindness and respect.

On the Sunday before my husband's tour bus arrived in Atlanta, I attended a service with my sister-in-law at her large Protestant church. At the church service, I felt a little perplexed. My sister-in-law would lift her hand in the air when she was praying or singing. It was strange yet comforting to me, but I didn't understand what it meant. I figured that it was something that people at this church did, just like I would do the sign of the cross at a Catholic mass.

On the night before my husband came back from his choir trip to Florida, I felt a deep sense of dread. As I lay in bed that night, I knew that I couldn't bear the pain anymore. Instead of feeling loved, I felt despised. I started to cry, and I couldn't stop. I cried all night. With deep anguish, I purged myself of any feelings that I still had for my husband.

The next morning, I wondered if I had awoken my brother-in-law and his wife in the middle of the night because my husband's brother had awoken me by loudly playing a recording of the "Alleluia Chorus" by Handel. Even though I had not had a drink the night before, my head hurt as if I had a hangover. I did not appreciate the loud music. Maybe playing the loud music was his revenge for my crying all night. It was on that night, though, that I finally cried my last tear over my marriage.

After I returned home from Atlanta, I no longer grieved my marriage, but I was still in a deep depression. Thankfully, things were about to change.

Enlightenment

It was late summer in 1981. I was at home in my bedroom alone. Suddenly, I experienced an excruciating pain in my chest that wouldn't go away. I laid down in my bed, but the pain wouldn't stop. Finally, out of desperation, I cried, "God, if you exist, please take the pain away!" The second the words left my mouth, the pain disappeared. I was stunned and sat upon the edge of the bed, stupefied. It was my first realization that God really did exist. I went about the rest of the day as if it hadn't happened, but it was the first inkling of hope that I had experienced in a long time. I was still depressed and was battling suicidal thoughts after this incident, but I was very soon going to experience a revelation about the love of God.

On the metro bus rides to and from the University of Minnesota, I would often see the same man reading a Bible. I didn't know why it bothered me, but I would try not to sit close to him. It was strange that he always seemed to be there since I rode the bus at different times on different days. One day, though, I had an uncanny, weird, and very frightening experience. It eclipsed the weirdness that I felt when I noticed the man reading his Bible on the bus.

It happened on a sunny fall day in 1981 while I was riding the bus home from the university. I was contemplating about how I would kill myself. All of a sudden, I saw a figure out of the corner of my eye. Looking almost like a cartoon character, it was quickly moving around the bus. It could move from seat to seat without noise and at an incredible speed. As I watched it jump around, I noticed that others on the bus were oblivious to what I was seeing.

The troll-like being was short and grayish-green with a large, warty face. It was extremely ugly and had bulging dark eyes that dangled out of its eye sockets. It kept sticking its snake-like tongue out at me while laughing and pointing a long, bony finger at me. The finger terrifyingly seemed to almost touch my face. I couldn't hear it laugh, but I could tell that it was laughing at me. I was extremely frightened. I had never taken hallucinatory drugs, and this happened in broad daylight, so I thought that I must be really losing my mind.

Finally, the bus got to my stop. As I disembarked, I saw another being. Much taller than me, she had an ethereal beauty and was wearing a long, white dress. I wonder to this day who she was, maybe an angel, but I am not sure. It was as if she was waiting just for me to get off the bus. She was standing just to the left of me as I got off the bus and stepped onto the sidewalk.

Because I had such trouble looking people in the eye, I was amazed at myself for stopping and looking right into her brilliant eyes. In fact, I do not really remember much else about her except for her eyes. I am not even sure what color they were, but they were bright and emanated love. I was mesmerized. As I absorbed the light from her aura, pure love warmed my soul. I experienced an overwhelming feeling of worth that I had never experienced in my whole life. It was as if she was communicating to me, without using words, *the value of my existence.* For a moment, my despair totally lifted. After what seemed like a long time, I looked down, and when I looked up again, she was gone.

When I tell Christians this story, they sometimes recoil, concerned that it might have been a demon that I saw since I describe the beautiful being as female. It is possible that they just think that I am crazy. However, in the Bible, angels do not have gender as they are spiritual beings. They more often appear as masculine beings, for example, Michael the Archangel.

There are, however, mentions of feminine-looking angels in an Old Testament book. Zechariah 5:9 says, "Then I raised my eyes and looked, and there were two women, coming with the wind in their wings; for they had wings like the wings of a stork, and they lifted up the basket between earth and heaven." Women do not have wings, but angels are winged creatures. Another verse, Hebrews 13:2, says, "Be not forgetful to entertain strangers: for thereby some have entertained angels unawares." The verse doesn't mention that the strangers would only be male. I still don't know for sure if she was an angel, a person, or a vision. I can only describe what I saw and how it impacted me.

Still baffled, a little shaken, and pondering the reasons for the strange experiences, I walked home. I also questioned whether I had any sanity left in me. Was I crazy? Did it really happen? What did it mean?

When I entered the living room of my house, I looked down and saw a Bible laying on the coffee table. I didn't own a Bible, and I never saw my husband with one, so I was surprised and intrigued. I picked it up and walked over to the dining room table, and sat down. Brian, now six years old, wouldn't be home from school for another hour, so I decided to flip it open. When I did, the first page of the Book of Romans appeared. I started to read it, and in one sitting, I finished the whole book. Some verses leaped out at me as if God was personally speaking to me, so I read through the chapters again two more times.

I had studied the Bible during a religion class at the College of St. Catherine, but it seemed dry and boring at the time. This time, the words came alive, and I received and understood the message. I read that I was loved by God, that all have sinned, and that if I believed and confessed that Jesus died and rose from the dead for me, I would be saved. My husband's pastor had asked me if I was saved before our marriage, but I didn't understand what he meant back then. Now, I finally understood what the word *saved* meant. I wanted the shame and condemnation that I lived with every day for years to be gone, and I was willing to do what was needed to alleviate my pain. Although I didn't know it at the time, the group of verses that caught my attention is called the Roman Road to salvation.

The first verse on the Roman Road is Romans 3:23, "For all have sinned, and come short of the glory of God." Catholics are taught a lot about sin, and I didn't need to be convinced that I had sinned. Early in my marriage, I used to think that my husband was better than me. It strangely comforted me to read that he was equally guilty of sin, too.

The second Scripture on the Romans Road to salvation is Romans 6:23, "For the wages of sin is death; but the gift of God is eternal life through Jesus Christ our Lord." I understood that the wages of sin are death because, at this point in my life, all I could think about was death.

Then I read Romans 5:8, "But God demonstrates His own love toward us, in that while we were still sinners, Christ died for us." The next verse is Romans 10:9, "That if you confess with your mouth Jesus as Lord, and believe in your heart that God raised Him from the dead, you will be saved." Although I didn't fully understand the gift that was being offered to me by God at that moment, I knew that I needed it. I wasn't going to question God or rail at Him anymore. I got down on my knees and asked Him for forgiveness of all my sins and asked Jesus to come into my life. At that moment, I felt a load of guilt lift and a comforting peace come over me.

My salvation experience would be just the beginning of my enlightenment. I had so much to overcome yet in my life. Even though I still had the same issues and problems in my life, at least I now had a new feeling of peace in my heart. The world seemed somewhat brighter, and even colors seemed more vivid. I had new hope, but I had so much to learn. I decided to add the Bible to my list of things to study, and then I tried to begin my life anew.

The people in Prague were also beginning their lives anew after the Velvet Revolution. They were beginning to experience their first taste of freedom, and like me, they were very hesitant and unsure of themselves.

Second Day in Prague

June 1990, Prague, Czechoslovakia

While strolling towards Wenceslas Square on the second day in Prague, I noticed some people singing American songs at a small pub. Even though very few people in Prague could speak English, these people appeared to love American music. Singing American songs seemed to symbolize their desire to adopt Western ideas and values in their country. One of the songs that I heard was *This Land is Your Land* by Woody Guthrie.

A street vendor at Wenceslas Square was selling some American items, such as Mickey Mouse and California Beach T-shirts, small American flags, and even miniature replicas of the Statue of Liberty. American flags were flying on some buildings. The people in Prague were having a love affair with the United States.

Street Vendors in Prague

In 1990, I knew that America had changed quite a bit since World War II. The last time that the Czecho-slovakian people had contact with Americans, though, was during and just after World War II. The people in Prague were really in love with America's past generation, the generation that they knew from World War II. They would have been shocked to have known that communist ideas were gaining steam in some American universities.

Some of the people believed that if they adopted American ideology, they would become rich. When I had an interpreter with me, I was asked a number of times about my car ownership. I responded each time that I had two cars. They were all flabbergasted. One man asked me if I could make Czechoslovakia a state of the United States. Owning cars was a symbol of wealth and prestige to the people.

Keeping some small American flags in my large purse, I was planning on giving them to any children that I might meet on my journey. Strangely, I didn't notice children congregating and playing together anywhere, except at the park that I strolled by not too far from Wenceslas Square. It was a small park that was dotted with benches and tucked between some residential areas. The smell of fresh green grass surrounded me as I walked under tall oak and maple trees in the park to get closer to the children. As I stopped and watched the children play, I noticed a few adults standing close by, conversing amongst themselves.

When I started to further approach the children, the adults noticed me and looked at me quizzically. I pulled out the flags from my purse and motioned towards the children. Immediately the adults began to smile and nod at me. The children quickly ran towards me, realizing that I was going to be giving them one of the flags.

I handed out the flags, surrounded by the smiling yet very quiet and polite children. I believe that they were trained to keep quiet in order to avoid any scrutiny of the family by the communist authorities. After I gave each child a flag, they held their new gift as if they cherished it. They joyously jumped up and down, looking at their own flag and comparing it to the one another child held. Realizing that I was from the United States, the adult guardians were eager to shake my hand. It was an amazing experience, and I realized how blessed that I was to be an American.

As I walked throughout Prague, I noticed that there were many churches in the city. In the Jewish section of the city, a large synagogue also exists. However, the main historical religion of Prague is Catholicism. Many religious statues and churches exist all over the city. The communists did not destroy any of the religious artifacts because they were considered important for historical value. Shutting down the churches, though, was one of the first things that the communists did. Freedom to worship in them was then denied.

In June of 1990, there appeared to be a revival of religious interest in Prague. Besides the American wares, I noticed another street vendor selling religious items such as crosses and small statues of the Virgin Mary. People were even attending church services on weeknights.

As I walked back to my hotel after my exploration of the city later that day, I noticed people entering a Catholic church. I decided to follow them. The church was packed, and the mass had already begun. Any late-comers, including me, stood at the back of the church. I was perplexed as to why so many people were going to church on an ordinary Monday afternoon. As I looked at the people's faces in the church, though, it dawned on me that the people were hungry for meaning in their lives. Some of the people had drawn faces showing a weariness of life. I could relate to their depression after what I had felt earlier in my own life.

Small Catholic Church in Prague

I learned later that young men were enrolling in the seminary in greater numbers than ever before. Even the schools would begin teaching religion again. Later, I heard a man explain, "When a dog is let off of his chain, he jumps up and runs around celebrating his freedom." It made sense to me. People do not like to be controlled and, by nature, will want to do whatever has been forbidden to do. Going to mass on a Monday was an act that celebrated the freedom to attend a church service again.

As I mulled over my experiences and observations in Prague, I realized that Karl Marx was wrong to assume that beliefs would change under communism. Marx believed that beliefs follow the mode of production. He believed that since materialism was much more important than philosophy or religion, people would appreciate the communist way of life and gladly accept its atheism. After forty-plus years of communist rule, though, it was apparent that some of the people still had differing religious and political beliefs within them. Communism failed to create a secular utopia. Instead, the tyranny of the imposed communist ideology impeded prosperity and created emptiness of soul, fear, unhappiness, and resentment in the people.

One person in Prague, however, had experienced freedom in his heart a long time ago. Because he had faith, wisdom, and courage, he also helped birth the Velvet Revolution. I was about to meet him.

The Physics Professor

On the third day in Prague, I was kindly invited to come along and meet the Czech cousin of the anesthesiologist in my tour group. The anesthesiologist had told me that his cousin was a professor who had participated in the Velvet Revolution. I was very intrigued and decided to join them. The anesthesiologist, his family, and I walked to meet him at one of the university's buildings not far from our hotel. I was very surprised when we approached him. Instead of an older, stuffy intellectual as I expected, I met a much more vibrant and youthful man.

The anesthesiologist first introduced himself and his family to his cousin. I enjoyed seeing the warmth between the cousins as they greeted each other, knowing that this was the first time that they had met each other. Then the professor turned toward me. As I shook his hand, I told him my name. I explained, "I am on an independent study from my university in St. Cloud, Minnesota, and so thrilled to be able to meet you and hear your story about the Velvet Revolution." He smiled at me while looking me in the eye and politely said in perfect English, "It is so very nice to meet you. I am in deep admiration of America." Then he said to all of us, "I am happy to tell you all about the events that led to our freedom."

After our introductions, the professor began his story. When he spoke, I noticed a brightness in his eyes and heard confidence in his voice. I intently listened as he explained that he had been a leader of a student protest group during the Prague Fall protests, as he called the student demonstrations prior to the start of the Velvet Revolution. He was also a leader during the first protest of the Velvet Revolution on November 17, 1989.

Fair, medium-built, and handsome, the professor also looked much too young to be a seasoned professor at Charles University. He couldn't have been much over thirty years old. He was pleasant and humble, yet he had a charismatic demeanor. He spoke English very well, and it was easy for me to follow his story. Impressed by his accomplishments at such a young age, I was speechless. I didn't ask any questions. I just listened. He was composed and articulate, and I was very moved by his story. I had sat in lecture halls previously and been bored by many professors, but this professor totally engaged me.

He was a professor of nuclear physics at Charles University. Before the Velvet Revolution, he had created an underground newspaper. This paper not only spoke out against communism but also provided news from outside the country. Prior to the 1989 revolution, the news media in the country had been totally controlled by the communist state. People behind the Iron Curtain were also forbidden to listen to outside news or ideas. Since he was a professor, this young man was able to travel outside the country on behalf of the university. As a result, he could hear the news that was forbidden by the communists.

The professor asked us if we would like to take a walk with him to the site of the first Velvet Revolution protest in Wenceslas Square. We gladly agreed. Describing the events that took place at the November 17th memorial rally for the medical student named Jan Opletal, the professor led us down National Street. Before we reached Wenceslas Square, he stopped us momentarily and said, "On the evening of the memorial to the student killed in 1939 by the Nazis during a protest rally, we marched down this very street toward Wenceslas Square. The group was comprised of hundreds of students and teachers on strike from the university."

As we approached the spot where he had been beaten by the police in the square, the professor stopped us again and explained, "We were ambushed by police here in the late afternoon. The police had cordoned us off so we couldn't escape. They beat us with clubs while police dogs mauled us. The police attacks went on for three hours. After the beatings were over, we were bloody and bruised. Then we were taken to police headquarters for intense interrogation. Many protesters were seriously hurt and are still recovering. Although nobody was killed, it could have happened. We were very fearful for the next few days as we hid from the police, believing that they would come for us and possibly even execute some of us. However, the unbelievable happened, for instead of being arrested, the whole city came out in support of our actions. Now we are heroes!" I was amazed. Death had stared them in the face, but he and the students had overcome their fear and had the courage to stand up to their oppressors.

The professor then led us to a plaque that had just been placed at the site of the beating. Moved from its original location, it is now located on the outside wall of a building on a backstreet near the National Theater in Wenceslas Square. It has concrete hands reaching out of it. The professor called it *The Empty Hands Symbol of Nonviolence*. One of the hands shows the "V" peace symbol.

The nonviolence and orderly behavior, even during the protests, were the expressed attitudes of the Czechoslovakian students. I believe that because each protest was orderly and nonviolent, the ideas promoted in them were more convincing to others not yet participating in the protests. The nonviolent protests in Czechoslovakia were just as powerful in gaining the support of the people as were the nonviolent Martin Luther King led marches in the United States during the civil rights era in the 1960s. It was good behavior from the protesters that inspired the uninvolved citizens. The citizens witnessed the great contrast between the protesters' behaviors and the undeserved violent reaction from the communist police. As a result, the whole country then fully supported the protesters.

The professor was also a member of the Salesian Order of the Catholic church. He was a priest as well as a professor. The Salesian order had originally been established in the nineteenth century to help children during the Industrial Revolution. His beliefs were very important to him. At first, his motivation to start the underground newspaper at the university was to promote his Christian beliefs. He had been upset that Czech Bibles had not been printed in thirty-five years, and he wanted to share his ideas and Christian beliefs with the students at the university. After he started traveling outside the country, he also wanted to share news from the outside world with the students. He did not realize that his next actions would help foment a revolution.

Every time the professor traveled outside of the country, he smuggled back into the country, piece by piece, parts for a copy machine. When he smuggled in the last piece of the machine, he put it together. With full control over a copy machine, he was able to publish his writings and distribute them more widely to the students at the university.

I was in awe of his bravery. Before the Velvet Revolution, he had risked his life every time he smuggled in a piece of that copy machine into the country. Remembering my fear when I crossed the border from Austria into Czechoslovakia, I imagined that he must have been very nervous each time he came back into the country, knowing that he could be imprisoned or killed for what the communists would consider to be treasonous actions. He had also risked his life every time he distributed his writings amongst the students.

At the time of my interview with the professor, he told me of his plans to quit teaching at the university. He wanted to establish a free newspaper. A book that influenced this young revolutionary is called *Conscience and Captivity: Religion in Eastern Europe*.[34] A contemporary author in 1990, she had graduated from Oxford University in England. Writing about the history of religion in each of the countries in Eastern Europe behind the Iron Curtain, she described how people of faith interacted with the state. She said, "East European believers have hammered some good out of evil, taught people to find inner freedom within tight political and economic constrictions, and nourished hope in an apparently hopeless situation."[35] Karl Marx would have had a lot of trouble with this book and this young professor. Faith, truth, and courage were the weapons that he had used to help bring down the ruthless communist regime in his country.

When I returned to the Czech Republic in 2019, I tried to find the professor turned writer. I wasn't able

34 Braun, 1988
35 Amazon, 2021

to find even where he had last taught at Charles University because I had failed to write down his name. I had also lost the contact information from his cousin. I do not know what happened to him. But his heroic life and story had such an effect on me that I would have very much liked to have met him again. He was a profound example that one person can make a difference for good. He had faith, courage, and he defied tyranny. He also inspired me not to accept lies and fight the tyranny in my own life.

I would also have liked to ask the professor more about his Christian beliefs and how and why he had become a believer. Even though he was a Catholic, and I had left the Catholic church, I knew that his faith in God was real. His journey in life was much different than mine, but we both had come to the same conclusion that following Jesus offers a path that leads to fulfillment and purpose in life.

Prague University Students

After the Velvet Revolution in November of 1989, the students were demanding change at the universities. Before the revolution, in order to become a university student, one either had parents in the Communist Party, or the parents had to bribe the authorities. Occasionally, an extremely intelligent child would be allowed to attend. College was not free for everyone.

Even though the Communist Party had complete control over the educational system and over who was allowed to attend, it is interesting to note that the students and professors were the ones that instigated the Velvet Revolution. The initial protests voiced opposition to the suppression of free thought by the government. Free expression of ideas was the main motivation.

In June of 1990, I found this quote by Tomas Machacek, a research student at the time, in a Czechoslovakian magazine called *Czechoslovak Life*.

Official propaganda always presented people who thought otherwise and who admitted it publicly as figures isolated from the silent majority. Suffice it to imagine that you are also part of the silent majority and keep quiet because you don't want to be an isolated figure and face all sorts of problems. Then, raising yourself above the personal level, you realize that the silent majority is made up of people who feel the same, and think the same, and keep quiet for the same reason.

To the community of twenty-year-olds, this was clear. They played the game of their elders, but they played it only because they wanted to be left alone and cultivate their own opinions surrounded by a shell. In the meantime, the generation of their parents continued to play the game, convinced that there was no chance of a change. Suddenly, the shell broke, and there was no need for explanations. The demands raised by the students were so just that disagreeing with them would have meant laying oneself open to ridicule.

Translated from the Czech language into English, I had to read it a couple of times before I understood his point. His main idea was that people under forced ideology are forced to claim publicly that they believe in those ideas; however, they do not believe them in their hearts. The people then keep silent to protect themselves and their families. They want to avoid all kinds of problems, such as being singled out by the group-think mob.

Since the students were raised in this oppressive environment, they also knew how to play the game just as well as their parents. When the students realized communally at the university that they all thought the same way, the student's passions for change were ignited. The knowledge that they all had the same negative view of communist ideas propelled the students' demands and demonstrations. Finally, once expressed openly during the demonstrations, the students' ideas for change were considered just and accepted by the general population.

Individualism

Changes were being made in Charles University in 1990. There were differing opinions on how to proceed in the future, though. The only thing achieved so far was the abolishment of the old authoritarian system. Since Marxist philosophy and preparatory military training were being abolished, a new philosophy had to emerge. University leaders wanted a curriculum that would encourage an individual approach instead of following the cookie-cutter approach of learning that had been prescribed for all under communism.

In adopting an individual approach to accommodate for different aptitudes and interests, a new curriculum format needed to be adopted to accomplish those goals. The most important aspect of the new law was to upend the idea of collectivism. Collectivism is a political theory that states that society as a whole is the unit of moral value. The opposite of collectivism is individualism, where the individual is considered the most important unit of moral value. Individualists value independence and self-reliance. They believe that each individual has value and should be protected.

They also oppose external interference into an individual's beliefs by government and society.

Instead of collectivism, the students in Prague wanted to uphold the rights of the individual. Each student now would have the right to select classes, teachers, schools and have the right to democratically elect academic officials. Also, access to world literature and the ability to learn any foreign language was important to them.

One anonymous medical student in 1990 said, "The New Year address by our new president had a profound effect on me. He convinced me that we must all begin with ourselves. I was never an excellent student, but I have decided to work hard because I see that people's initiative is a thing that will count from now on." As the ideology of individualism was being reintroduced into the universities, the ideas of communism and collectivism were being abolished. The two belief systems cannot coexist. Individual motivation for success leads to hard work and the improvement of knowledge and skills. It also fuels optimism and productivity. The same can't be said about communism.

New Idealism in Prague

In 1990, the attitudes in the city of Prague were unique in Czechoslovakia. I found idealism and optimism much more pronounced here than in the other cities that I visited. People seemed more hopeful for a better life under the new republic. Optimism was higher here because Prague is where the revolution began. The people had also seen more extensive outward changes than anywhere else in Czechoslovakia. With a new president, freed expressions of speech, and improvements to the infrastructure already underway, the people had reason for hope. They sincerely believed that with hard work and the new ideology of individualism, the people would soon become prosperous and happy.

When I returned to Prague in 2019, the economy was alive and well. The city was booming economically. There were new and restored buildings, and everything was alive with color. There were many thriving small businesses. Most of the restaurants and shops that I saw in 2019 didn't exist when I was there in 1990. Tourism has become a major source of revenue. The streets were also alive with traffic, so I assume that many people now have at least one car to call their own, their symbol of wealth in 1990.

As I left the city of Prague in 1990, I thought about the people that I met and the stories that I heard. I realized that ideology is so important, not just to a country but also to the individuals within a country. Like the medical student who became more motivated to study after the Velvet Revolution, I was also becoming more motivated to learn. Initially, when my in-laws suggested that I go and get a job, I hadn't planned on going back to college. After I couldn't find a job, my motivation to get a college degree was then propelled by a desire to make a decent wage. In other words, my motivation was not my own. I felt controlled by my family, and the students felt controlled by the Soviet system. We both are examples that prove that control does not positively motivate people. As I compared my life to this student's life, I realized that the oppression in my own life must also be overcome before I could truly thrive. I realized that an external force cannot ignite in a person the motivation to learn and cultivate his or her abilities.

It was in Prague where I found my internal motivation. While I did get good grades in college, I really didn't have a passion for learning. In Prague, I gained a passion for continuing my studies. When I got back home, I began to look for a doctorate program. The example of the professor and of the others that I met during this trip changed the way that I saw myself. I was inspired to fight the lies in my life that said that I was not valuable. I wasn't depressed since my salvation experience, but it wasn't until I took this trip that I realized that I had only been existing and not really living.

Before I went to sleep the night before we left Prague, I also thought about the most important people in my life, my children. In 1990, I had three children at home. I wanted to be a good role model to them. My heart ached to be back with them and hug them. I was often so busy, and I knew that they often felt alone since I had gone back to college. I knew that they needed more nurturing and training than I was giving them. Unfortunately, I was not a confident person, so I couldn't teach them how to be confident. I still needed to grow in wisdom. Even though I felt freer after my spiritual conversion, I was still a very timid and easily controlled person. I still had not broken the shackles of discouragement and the feelings of inferiority that had kept me bound since childhood.

When I climbed into bed that night, I was not sleepy. Instead, I thought about my own childhood, my children, and the events that led me back to college for the third time.

Reflection on My Childhood

As I grew older in my childhood during the early 1960s, I had become numb inside toward my family. I did not feel a loving connection to them. I had also stopped reacting normally to some events.

One time, when I was about eleven or twelve years old, I was with my family visiting my aunt Jean's cabin. The cabin was on the other side of the larger lake near our farm. It took only ten minutes to drive to the cabin. In the summer, we would often go to the cabin on a Sunday afternoon to waterski. My aunt Jean's husband had a small fishing boat, but we were allowed to use it to waterski when we were visiting. The motor was only strong enough to pull the lighter children out of the water, so I learned to waterski at a fairly young age. The lake was spring-fed and cold. Most of the older people weren't very interested in swimming or waterskiing because of the coldness of the water, except for my aunt Jean.

Aunt Jean was an energetic, boisterous person who was full of opinions, but she also had a great sense of humor. She was my father's first cousin, but I knew her as my aunt. I enjoyed listening to her make cracks at or about the men in the family. She seemed to be somewhat of a woman's libber. She would pick on the men for their faults and for what she saw as male privilege, but she always did it with a gleam in her eye.

After waterskiing one afternoon, I changed into dry clothes in one of the back bedrooms and went to sit down at the small kitchen table. The cozy cabin had two bedrooms, a bathroom, a small kitchen, and a tiny living area. As I sat down, my aunt sat a plate of chocolate chip cookies in front of me, loudly asking me if I wanted one. Without thinking, I shook my head, implying no. She then asked me if a cat had my tongue. I just sat there frozen. I didn't think that I was allowed to have cookies at home, so I wouldn't accept a cookie at my aunt's cabin. I felt uncomfortable with the situation, so I left the table and went outside.

I was conditioned throughout my childhood to feel unworthy, and therefore, I wouldn't accept a cookie. I became an easier target for predatory people. I believe that it was the reason that I was a target of molestation and rape as a teenager. As a child, my heart was filled with pain and loneliness, and I would sometimes cry myself to sleep. During the day, though, I wore a smiling mask and was eager to please. I was trying to accept the lie that my childhood was fine. Living a lie is an open door for the spirit of tyranny to invade and control your life. Agreeing with a tyrannical spirit is a contract for insanity and self-destruction.

My pleasant childhood memories at home occurred when I was alone during any free time that was allowed. Those times helped me keep what sanity that I still had intact. They mostly involved my family's dog and horse and the quiet wilderness of the north. I loved to escape the angry farmhouse any chance that I could. I would often go riding on our quarter horse through the fields and woods with our family dog, Cookie, running alongside. I would even take the horse out on cold, winter days. The horse couldn't go fast through the snow, but I didn't care. I just liked getting away from the farmhouse.

As a young child, I did not like getting up early at five o'clock in the morning to milk the cows in the middle of the winter. However, I don't have bad memories of the cold itself when I was outside. The shock of being awakened to the quiet, star-filled, pre-dawn sky was exhilarating. As I breathed in the crystallized air, I would also feel its invisible, sharp needles stinging any exposed skin on my face, which was not covered by my scarf. As I quickly walked to the barn, I could see my frozen breath leave me as I crunched the snow underneath me in my rubber barn boots. Sometimes, during blizzard-like conditions, it would be hard to see in front of me at all. Our dog would happily accompany us to the barn, which would make me wonder how our dog, cats, horses, and cows could stay alive outside in the frigid temperatures. The cows would usually be huddled right next to the barn as they tried to shield themselves from any wind in the sometimes forty-degree below zero weather. I was so grateful that I didn't have to sleep outside.

One of the chores that I didn't mind as a teenager was burning the trash at night. I spent many of those nights watching the Northern Lights dance across the sky while I poked the fire pit with a stick to make sure the fire burned everything capable of burning. Charred tin cans would litter the area when the fire went out.

While I awaited the trash to finish burning, I would wonder about what lay ahead in my life as I watched the eerie, many-hued light show. I would dream of having my own family, imagining a healthy, happy home, and escaping the tyranny of my childhood. I loved Disney movies, so I imagined a happy ending to my childhood. I would wonder about the handsome prince that would be in my future. A prince that I was sure would eventually rescue me from my unhappy childhood and create a beautiful family with me. I truly didn't understand then that a man would not be the answer to my problems. I didn't know that I had to learn how to rid myself of tyranny before I could truly be happy.

The degree of tyranny in a person's life can be gauged by the attitudes it causes. Anger, resentment, unhappiness, hopelessness, and fear are the side effects of tyranny. I remember gritting my teeth a lot, trying to avoid showing any negative feelings just as my dad did. Those pent-up feelings destroy a person's self-worth, lead to a negative view of life, and destroy potential achievements. At the time, I felt alone, but I know that there are many other people who have grown up inside a tyrannical home. I know that many of those people had it much worse than I.

By 1981, I had now lived through more pain as an adult. Even after my salvation experience at age twenty-nine, the tyranny in my life still existed. That same year, I become pregnant again. My dream of having a happy family had been reborn, but I was still a very insecure person. I still needed to learn how to become who I was meant to be. I now felt valuable, but I did not have much wisdom. There was much yet to learn.

Kathleen

May 1982, Minneapolis, Minnesota

The six-year period between my salvation experience in 1981 and our move out of Minneapolis in 1987 was the happiest time for me in my young adult life. I still didn't know what was going on inside of my husband, though, and I still felt numb toward him. We had joined a medium-sized church in St. Paul, Minnesota. My husband was the worship leader for the church and was well-liked by the pastor because of his beautiful tenor voice. I was involved in the children's ministries, mainly taking care of the two and three-year-old children. My husband seemed to want to rekindle his childhood Christianity, so I erroneously made the presumption that our marriage would eventually get better.

My second child, Kathleen Marie, was born on May 5, 1982, eight months after my salvation experience. We nicknamed her Katie. Her birth was amazing. I had a C-Section because the doctors guessed that she was a month overdue and too big to go through the birth canal.

During the surgery, I was wide awake and propped up slightly on an operating table and situated behind a sheet wall so that I couldn't see the doctor cut me. I had been given spinal block anesthesia, so I didn't feel any pain. The white operating room was very cold and the smell of antiseptic cleaners hung in the air.

When the doctor pulled Katie out of me, she didn't cry. At that same moment, I felt an incredible feeling of overwhelming love wash over me. It was as if angels had appeared in the room to applaud her birth. Her eyes showed her shock, though, and they opened as wide as her mouth.

After the nurse wrapped her and put her in my arms, I kissed her forehead and snuggled her while whispering, "Hi Katie." She amazingly lifted her head off of my shoulder to look at me. Being way overdue, she was a large baby, weighing almost ten pounds. Still, I was shocked that she could lift her head. Afterward, she nuzzled back into my shoulder. I was overwhelmed with joy. When I took her home from the hospital, I noticed that the lilacs were blooming all over the city. The fragrance and beautiful purple flowers appropriately symbolized my new happiness.

Right before Katie's birth, I had quit college for the

second time. I decided to stay home and be a full-time mom. Even though we were poor, we somehow managed to get by. I enjoyed being a stay-at-home mom. I tried to help Brian become more secure.

Katie was very easy to care for as she was a very sweet baby and toddler. I didn't want to miss all those moments with her that I had missed with Brian when he was in childcare. I certainly did not want either of us to suffer the horrible pain of separation. I tried to follow all the teachings from the Bible about being a good wife. I was more attentive to the needs of my family, tried to make great lunches and dinners, and tried to be a respectful wife.

My husband and I didn't fight as much, but there was still a great chasm between us. We still did not truly communicate.

David

1985-86, Minneapolis, Minnesota

In spite of my dysfunctional marriage, when Katie was three, I was ready to try to have another child. In the fall of 1985, I found out that I was pregnant when I had an early miscarriage. A month afterward, I got pneumonia and had to have an X-ray done.

As I stood in front of the X-ray machine, the lab technician asked me, "Are you pregnant?" I didn't think that I could be with child so soon after a miscarriage, so I said, "No." A couple of weeks later, though, I suspected that I was pregnant because I experienced morning sickness. Soon afterward, I went to my doctor, and it was confirmed. I was going to have a baby. I was very happy, but the happiness was short-lived.

When I was about three months along, I had my first ultrasound. The lab doctor reviewed my results and came into my room. He said, "We have discovered a problem with your baby. I have called your doctor's office, and they are requesting that you go there immediately." At first, the news hit me hard. I wondered, "What could be wrong with my baby?" I was alone since my husband did not join me for any doctor or lab visits, so I internalized my anxiety as usual.

After I left the lab, I fearfully got into my car and drove to my obstetrician's office. After I arrived, I did not have to wait very long before being called in to see the doctor. When I walked into her office, she sympathetically greeted me.

My doctor was a kind, attractive person in her early thirties. She was of medium height and had green eyes and long, light brown hair. I sat down, feeling somewhat numb, not sure what the doctor would say to me. She took a deep breath while her eyes communicated to me that the news was not good. She finally said, "Your baby has severe hydrocephalus."

I had heard the term before, but I truly didn't understand its implications. She went on to say, "Hydrocephalus is a condition that causes excess fluid to fill the brain cavities in the baby, causing the skull to be abnormally formed." After she was done with her explanation, I sat still, but thoughts were wildly erupting in my head. I didn't fully understand or accept everything that she was saying, but in my shock, I had no ability to question the news.

It was suggested that I schedule an abortion, but that went against my beliefs. If I didn't have an abortion, I was told that my baby would still die because of the serious birth defect. My doctor seemed to understand that I needed time to digest what I had just been told, so she said, "Please, take some time to think and talk it over with your husband." I nodded okay, even though I knew that I wouldn't discuss having an abortion with my husband.

Before I left the office, the doctor gave me some information to read through at home. Feeling shocked and very sad, I scheduled another appointment.

I went home and read through the pamphlets. The complication for me involved giving birth to a baby with severe hydrocephalus. The baby would not make it to full gestation. I would most likely carry him for only six months. Due to the baby's inability to swallow amniotic fluid because of the birth defect, the fluid would continue to build in my uterus until I went into labor prematurely. Since he would not be able to go through the birth canal because his head would not be fully formed, I would have to deliver him by C-section. Having a C-section at that stage of the pregnancy can cause the mother to hemorrhage with a serious risk of death.

Even though I finally understood the risk, I was unable to agree to have an abortion. I had always been pro-life, even before my spiritual conversion, but now my belief would be put to the test. Instead of having an abortion, I decided to put my life in God's hands. I surrendered to God whether I would live or die. I only knew that I could not live with myself if I had an abortion. I was also hoping for a miracle cure for my baby.

The weeks being pregnant with David were difficult. As the time drew near, I experienced strange swooshing sensations in my enlarged belly. Sometimes it scared me because I hadn't experienced the same sensations during my other pregnancies. I grew large so fast that I thought my stomach was going to explode. I prayed and cried often. I didn't talk to my husband about my feelings, though. I felt alone and kept asking God the question, why?

I wanted to have this baby, and I wanted him to be healed. I remember one day that I cried so hard that I thought I would never stop. I wasn't angry with God, but I didn't understand why I was going through this. A verse in the Bible, Isaiah 55:8, states, "For my thoughts are not your thoughts, neither are your ways my ways." I certainly didn't understand what God was thinking about my situation.

As time went on, the healing that I was praying for didn't come. As my belly got larger, I got more fearful and wondered what good could possibly come from this experience. Every time I went into the doctor's office, though, I would feel a calm come over me. I knew that the people in the office cared about my baby and me. I sensed grace lifting me and giving me rest from the fearful times that I would have at home. I was learning that faith in God involves trusting that He is in control, even if what happens is not what I want. I was learning that life would still have tragedies as well as miracles, sadness as well as happiness. As Ecclesiastes 3:1 says, "There is a time for everything and a season for every activity under the heavens."

God did not heal David, but He was present when David was born. I know that God is everywhere, but sometimes He makes His presence known in amazing ways. Like Moses and the burning bush, He can visibly appear suddenly. I believe that God never changes. Whatever miracles, great or small that have been done in the past can and do happen today.

When I went to the hospital to have a C-section

on June 6, 1986, I went in knowing that it might be my last day on earth. As I lay on the operating table, stripped naked before they put me under, I silently asked God to be with me, my baby, Katie, and Brian.

As the doctors finished prepping me for surgery, my focus narrowed as I wondered if I would soon meet face to face with God. I wondered about Jesus being nailed to the cross. My arms were outstretched and restrained just like His arms had been before the Roman guards plunged the first nail into Him. In my naked state, I felt uncomfortable and exposed. For Him, being naked was the least of His agony. Before I could think anymore, my world went dark.

I didn't come out of unconsciousness until the next day. I had hemorrhaged. As the hemorrhage was expected, I had been immediately given a blood transfusion which saved my life. When I awoke, I was surprised that my mom was with me. I never expected to see her, and I didn't say much to her. My husband was with Katie and Brian, so I forgave him for not coming to see me.

Later that same afternoon, I was taken to another wing of the hospital to meet my son, David. There were a lot of babies in that sterile, cold, and bright white intensive care unit. There was also a flurry of activity with doctors and nurses all busy with many premature babies. As I was rolled on my hospital bed toward David's incubator, I wondered what I would see. They stopped me right next to my baby. He lay in his incubator and was attached to a device to help him breathe.

Even though he was three months premature, he seemed much bigger than the neighboring premature babies. He was long, thin, and perfect, except for his skull. The bones of his skull never fully formed. I chose to ignore his imperfection and just looked at his eyes. I quietly whispered, "Hi David." I also put my finger in his little hand. He seemed to recognize my voice. He slightly squeezed my finger, and his eyes looked back at mine. I felt an overwhelming love for him. I couldn't have loved him more if he had come out more perfect.

After a few minutes, the doctor in charge of David asked me, "Are you ready to hold him?" I knew that it meant that they would take him off of the respirator machine. I nodded okay, and they took the respirator out of his mouth and handed him to me. He was so frail, and then as I held him, I felt his little body crumple. It was as if he lost a little weight in that second.

At that same moment, though, something incredible happened. A shiny mist enveloped the room. Everything went quiet for a moment. It was as if, for a couple of seconds, time stopped. I sensed Jesus standing near me, taking my son out of my arms to be with Him. I felt such an immense peace. I knew that David was safe in a better place. I know that I will see my baby again.

Even though I accepted David's death, I still grieved his loss. I had empty-arms syndrome after I came home from the hospital. We had a funeral, and that gave me some comfort. My husband openly cried at the gravesite, which was the only time that I saw him express emotion. We didn't grieve together.

What I know now about marriage is that communication is very important. I believe that the lack of communication in my marriage led to many misunderstandings. Those misunderstandings birthed an ever-deepening resentment between us. We couldn't grieve together because we didn't even know or like each other.

David

September 1988, St. Cloud, Minnesota

When I went back to college at St. Cloud State University in September of 1988, one of my first classes was Speech, as it was a graduation requirement. I was very afraid of speaking in front of people, so it forced me to face one of my fears. The first assignment in the class was a debate. One student would give a pro-position and another student a con-position on issues of the day.

I was chosen to take the position of anti-abortion. It was an emotional topic for me after my experience with David's birth. As I wrote the speech, I decided to tell the story about my David.

When I stood before the class, an unknown confidence suddenly arose in me as I delivered the speech from my heart. Grace filled the room. As I shared how God was with me during my tragedy, I sensed that God was speaking to some of the students in the classroom. They all seemed to react to my speech positively. I even saw a couple of students shed a tear. My hope was that the message conveyed on that day was that God loves all people, born or unborn. Every individual does have value. Everyone, even the least of us, deserves dignity.

After the speech, I found it strange that I could communicate to strangers about my experience with David, but I could not talk to my own husband about it. If it wasn't for the comfort that God gave me on the day after David's birth, I believe that I could have lost heart.

Kristina

July 1987, Minneapolis, Minnesota

On July 10, 1987, thirteen months after David's birth, my youngest daughter, Kristina Mae, was born. At the same time, we were in the process of selling our house in Minneapolis. I was hoping that we could find a nicer house in the suburbs somewhere. We had started looking at houses, but at the same time, my husband and his parents were making a deal without my knowledge. My husband would build a house for us at his parent's farm in central Minnesota. In exchange for the land, a mother-in-law's apartment for them would be built in the basement of the new house so that they could come and go as they pleased in their retirement years.

I decided to accept our move to the farm without a fight. I was so happy to have an adorable new daughter. Her middle name, Mae, was the first name of my dad's mom. She was the only older relative in my life that I remember kindly noticing me when I was little.

I only remember seeing my grandmother a few times, but she left an impression on me. She would spend time with us children, taking us on walks to go blueberry picking during the northern Minnesota summer. Since she lived in Michigan, she didn't often visit when I was a child. She died when I was about eleven years old. It is amazing to me that I remember her treatment of me when I was little since I saw her so infrequently. Later in life, I would meet a man in Pilsen, Czechoslovakia, who would shed some light on why I distinctly remember her.

It seemed like a miracle to me that Kristina was healthy after experiencing a miscarriage and then the loss of David. My doctor, who was with me throughout my pregnancy with David, came out of her own pregnancy leave to deliver my daughter. I had to have another C-section, as back then, once a C-section, always a C-section.

At one of my office visits, my doctor told me, "I was so moved by the experience of delivering your baby boy. I want to be there when you deliver this next baby. However, I am also pregnant and due to deliver in the same month as you are, but if I can, I will be there to deliver your baby." She wanted to meet my new daughter and see my happy face when she handed her to me. Incredibly, she also told me that she would never do another abortion in memory of David.

On the day Kristina was born, my doctor indeed kept her promise. She delivered my baby. With a big smile, she handed Kristina over to me as I lay on a bed in the delivery room and said, "She is so beautiful. Congratulations, mom."

I cuddled Kristina after her birth, admiring her good looks. She was perfect, and much to my surprise, she had a full head of beautiful, brown hair. I hugged her and said, "Hi Kristina." She looked back at me with a quizzical look on her face. I don't think she was too happy about joining this cold world. I also realized that she must be very intelligent because of her expressions.

As I admired her, I realized how much I loved all of my children. Each child's birth was unique, but I felt the same love for each of my babies. Soon they whisked Kristina away, and I went into a recovery room. I was left to my own thoughts, so happy to have a healthy and adorable baby girl.

Moving Out of Minneapolis

We sold our house in south Minneapolis in October of 1987 for a twenty-thousand-dollar profit after a major remodeling effort. It seemed like a lot of money to me. My husband had been working little by little to modernize it since we bought the house in 1977. I helped strip paint from the woodwork and did some wall-papering and painting. The money we made on the sale of the house paid for our living expenses for a couple of months, and we bought building materials for my husband to start building the new house.

As I wrapped my dishes in paper and placed them into boxes, I thought about our move. I would not miss the old Minneapolis house, but I was also not looking forward to living in a small, old trailer during the cold, Minnesota winter. The trailer had been built in the 1950s for miners moving to northeastern Minnesota during the boom in iron ore mining on the Mesabi Iron Range.

The metal trailer sat on the farm property and would be our living quarters while the house was being built. It was cramped since it only contained one tiny bedroom. There were bunk beds in a small hall-

way between the kitchen and living area and the bedroom. A tiny bathroom with only a narrow shower was
sandwiched between the bedroom and the bunk beds.

There was no room in the tiny trailer for a crib for
Kristina. Her bed was a large dresser drawer in which
I placed a folded quilt for a mattress. I was up with
her at least two times a night since she wasn't sleeping
well. The yard light shined through the back window
into our little bedroom, and I think it caused her to
wake up. While sitting on the edge of the bed, I would
hold and nurse her until she went back to sleep.

By the mid-winter of 1988, Kristina had outgrown
the dresser drawer. It was such a relief to finally be
able to move out of the trailer and into the basement
of the house. Finally, I could set up the crib and our
queen size bed in the bedroom of the basement. The
two upper floors of the house were still being worked
on. Even so, I so appreciated the space that we now
had after living in the cramped trailer. The basement
had a furnace as well as a wood-burning stove to heat
the house. There was one bedroom, one bath, plus a
kitchenette and a fairly large living area. Eventually, it
would become the mother-in-law's apartment. Katie
and Brian were both sleeping in the living room until

my husband partially finished a bedroom for Brian on the main level of the house.

By the spring of 1988, I felt pressured to look for a job by my husband's parents. They were visiting the farm more often since they could now stay in the old trailer. I obediently started to look for a job, but I couldn't find one close to home. I decided that it would be best to go back to college and finally finish my college degree.

Because of our low income, I was able to get grants to help pay for school. I registered for classes at St. Cloud State University, which was only about a forty-minute drive from my home. I also took on a part-time job helping to take care of a disabled teenage girl to help bring in some money. I was allowed to take her to my home at times, so I could spend more time with my own children and maybe catch up on some laundry. She enjoyed being around my children, too.

A couple of years later, when I became a teacher's assistant at St. Could State University for my last year of my master's program, I got free tuition and a stipend which helped greatly. I also borrowed the maximum that I could from a government loan program. It seemed like the best way to ease our financial burden while I was finishing my degree. I thought that once I graduated, I would be able to get a good-paying job. I also thought that paying the loan back would not be an issue. I reasoned that if I had instead gotten a job and not gone back to school, I would not have made enough money to make working worthwhile, considering that child care costs would take a big chunk out of my income.

Prelude to My Trip

Spring, 1990, Central Minnesota

I graduated with a degree in Economics and Math from St. Cloud State University in December of 1989. I looked for a suitable job, but I found none available near my home. Instead, I decided to apply for an MBA, a master's program in Business Administration. The school didn't offer a master's degree in Economics, which was the subject that I loved, but I also thought that an MBA would be more marketable. During my first semester, I also found a part-time job as the director of a chamber of commerce for a neighboring city.

One day, while going through the mail at the chamber of commerce in the early spring of 1990, my eyes were drawn to a brochure mailed to my office from a small college in southern Minnesota. The brochure advertised a planned economic forum to be held in Prague, the capital of Czechoslovakia. It invited business and educational leaders to attend a two-week trip to build trade relationships between our two countries. As I read through the brochure, my interest grew. I felt a strange pulling in my spirit to investigate it further as if God was directing me.

With some hesitation, I called the number on the brochure to find out more details about the trip. I wasn't sure that it was doable, but my curiosity over-ruled my hesitancy. At first, I had blown off the idea since there were a few obstacles to overcome before I could attend the forum.

After I got the information for the trip, I wondered if I had time to arrange everything. I had to come up with the money, get permission from the board of the chamber of commerce to take the two weeks off, clear it with my husband, and arrange for the care of my three children while I was gone. They were daunting tasks since I was so busy all of the time. Besides the usual home responsibilities, attending two classes in my first semester of the MBA program, and my job at the chamber of commerce, if I were to attend the fo-rum, I would need to spend extra time arranging and financing the trip.

As I tried to brush the thought of going to Czecho-slovakia aside, a growing excitement permeated my soul. I wanted to go, and I became willing to do what-ever it took to get there. I approached my former pro-fessor of Economics, a believer in communism, and asked him if he would be willing to be my proctor for an independent study in Czechoslovakia. I showed him the brochure about the trip, and he was as intrigued as I was and agreed to be my professor for the independent study.

My professor was a thin, average-height man in his late thirties. He wore glasses, had a wry smile, and possessed a dry wit. He would stroke his fuzzy, brown beard when he was engrossed in thought. Easy-going but still commanding his class very well, he encouraged discussions on the social issues of our time, such as homelessness, drugs, and the first Iraq war.

During one session, a female classmate began profusely explaining why we needed to help the homeless. As I listened, I found myself agreeing that the homeless needed help, but I wasn't following her logic. She believed that homeless people drink too much because their situation is hopeless, and because they drink too much, they can't get a job. She thought that if the government provided everything for them, they would quit drinking and become productive members of society. I didn't agree. I wasn't sure that homelessness alone caused the drinking. There are other reasons why people drink too much.

Before I could hold myself back, I thought out loud, "So why do college students drink so much?" The class immediately burst into laughter, and a couple of the younger male students even laughingly fell out of their chairs. I immediately felt bad for the young woman when her face fell because she was so passionate about her ideas. She did not look my way. My socialist professor, though, still believed in critical thought. Even though I am sure that he empathized with the other student's ideas, he was open-minded enough to allow for discussion and a difference of opinions. He even chuckled at my outburst, so I thought that he would be the right person to be my proctor for the independent study. With the green light from my professor, I felt more confident that I was supposed to go.

Since I had borrowed the maximum amount from the government student loan program for my first quarter of the MBA program, I had extra money after paying for tuition and books. I had saved the money to use if my husband had a work dry spell, which was not uncommon for carpenters in the 1980s. It was enough money to pay for the trip. Thankfully, due to price controls under communism in Czechoslovakia, I was paying 1950s' prices for the tour expenses. The airfare was the biggest expenditure. The rest of the trip was very inexpensive.

I thought that my biggest obstacle in arranging the trip would be my husband. My husband rarely thought that any of my ideas were good. This time, though, he was surprisingly agreeable. I was able to easily arrange for the care of my children while I was gone. The neighbor who babysat my three-year-old daughter, Kristina, was willing to help out. She was like family and had once babysat for my husband when he was little. I knew that I could depend on her to help out if needed while I was gone.

Finally, all the arrangements were made. I finished up my two spring quarter classes with good marks and got ready to go on the trip. As the trip was drawing nearer, I was becoming more and more nervous, but I also had confidence that I was supposed to go.

Soon, I was actually on the trip, experiencing many amazing new things and still unaware of the total impact that it would have on my life.

Karlovy Vary

June, 1990, Karlovy Vary, Czechoslovakia

After visiting Prague, our tour bus headed toward Karlovy Vary. An important industrial city in Bohemia, it is also a spa town situated on the confluence of the Ohre and Tepla rivers. It is located about eighty miles west of Prague, so our bus trip did not take long. Karlovy Vary is named after the King of Bohemia, Charles IV, who founded the city in 1370.[36] Settlers from nearby Germany had moved to the area in the thirteenth century. Therefore, German was the main language in the city until 1945, when all German-speaking people were banished after World War II.[37]

The city has always been a significant tourism area and is known for its natural hot springs. It contains factories with a world-renowned reputation for making high-end china and exquisite crystal glassware. Kings and queens from all over Europe have purchased sets of both for their public and private use. The spas have hosted famous people from all over the world for centuries.

---

36 Wikipedia, 2021
37 Id.

As our tour bus drove into the city, I could tell that it was a place where the rich and elite liked to frequent. It was much smaller than Prague, but it emanated old wealth. Watching from my bus window, I noticed a magnificent, exotic-looking church with glistening gold domes in the hills above the city. I found out later that it was the Orthodox Cathedral of St. Peter and Paul built in the 1890s. The architecture of the church had been inspired by an older Russian Byzantine church near Moscow.

When we reached our destination, I immediately fell in love with the cozy elegance of the famous downtown spa area. After checking in to our hotel, I couldn't wait to go exploring. The downtown is divided by a small stream of the river, Tepla, and it is decorated with high-class hotels, restaurants, spas, and shops. The mostly Neo-Baroque and Neo-Renaissance-style buildings are about four stories high, but because of the mixture of architectural styles, no two buildings look alike. The downtown has fairy-tale-like qualities, such as river-crossing walking bridges on every block with sidewalks on both sides of the river. I almost expected to see a troll stopping us before walking to the other side.

Karlovy Vary Downtown Hotels

In 1370, the King of Bohemia and Holy Roman Emperor, Charles IV, had made the city famous. He found that the warm springs relieved his sore legs.[38] The word spread, and soon many people were visiting, hoping to be cured by the waters. People also drink the mineral water from the springs to help with digestive ailments. Some even claim that the waters have magical powers. The spas are the main attraction for most people visiting the city, but for me, the history of the city was much more fascinating.

When I first ventured out of the hotel, I decided to take a long walk. The trees rustled above me as I walked outside. I wore a sweater since it was a cool

38 Wikipedia, 2021

and windy day. I followed a sidewalk towards the Hotel Pupp, one of the most prestigious hotels in the spa area. A pathway near the hotel then led me to a scenic walkway that seemed to invite me to follow it. As I walked along the path, it led me towards a rocky hill. When I arrived just below the hill, I suddenly stopped. To my amazement, I saw a monument to Peter the Great situated on a rock beneath a gnarly oak tree. I was very surprised to see a monument to a Russian tsar in what was considered to be a German city back in his day. It is located below a famous lookout above the city called Peter's Height.

The sandstone bust of the tsar was created in 1877. In November of 1712, the Russian tsar had made a bet with a friend, saying that he could ride bareback to the top of one of the rocky hills. There was no trail, so it took great riding skills to reach the top. Afterward, it is said that he carved his initials into a large wooden cross that had stood on the site. In honor of that feat, the bust of Peter the Great was installed on a rock below the lookout.[39]

In 1990, the people of Karlovy Vary were busy giving a face lift to the centuries-old buildings. History is literally written on their buildings. As I walked by

39 Information Centre Karlovy Vary, 2021

one of the buildings near downtown, I saw the name, Goethe, chiseled into the outer wall of the building. I imagined that the famous German poet, Johann Wolfgang von Goethe, had lived there. The building sits near to the Grand Hotel Pupp, where the famous author's bust is also located. As I suspected, I learned later that Goethe had visited Karlovy Vary numerous times during his lifetime.

Later in the day, I joined the tour group to meet a local tour guide. He did not speak English, so the professor in our tour group translated for us. It was only an hour tour, so I didn't get the chance to ask him any personal questions.

As we strolled along the beautiful town center walkway, the sun was starting to set. The tour guide explained that he was ashamed of the terrible conditions of the buildings. His mood matched the approaching darkness and the increasing coldness of the air. I wrapped my sweater closely around my body as the temperature dropped while trying to listen intently to the interpretation of his words. He blamed the disrepair on the communist government. The government had not allowed the people to do any maintenance on the buildings for many years. I could feel disgust emanating from him as he spoke, but I also sensed in him a great love for his city.

The pride of his people, even though it was wounded by the rule of the communists, had truly never died. In 1990, it was time for a comeback. I witnessed the start of the renovations, seeing scaffolding being erected on some of the buildings for the repairs. The people were not wasting any time.

When we left Karlovy Vary the next day, I thought about the people that I had met so far on my trip. One thing was in common. A great resentment toward the communists existed in all of them. Their dignity had been stolen from them by the communists when they lost their identity as independent people.

The Minister of Transportation

June 1990, Pilsen, Czechoslovakia

The next stop in our journey was the fascinating city of Pilsen in western Bohemia. It is located about ninety kilometers from Prague. Famous for Pilsner lager, the beer was invented here in 1842.[40]

The Skoda factory also exists here. In the past, the Skoda factory-made locomotives, and it also made tanks for the Nazis during World War II. After the communist government took control of Czechoslovakia, they initially renamed the factory Lenin Works, after Vladimir Lenin, the first leader of Soviet Russia. Humorously, they changed the name back to Skoda after Germany returned purchased goods. The Germans hated the communist name, Lenin Works, and would not purchase any more goods from the factory unless the name was changed.[41]

The Skoda factory also made reactors for nuclear power in 1990.[42] Now the factory makes many cars. In 2019, I saw many Skoda cars while driving a rented

40 Wikipedia, 2021
41 Id.
42 Id.

Skoda along the highways and cities throughout the Czech Republic. It was quite a contrast to the empty roads that I witnessed in 1990.

On my first day in Pilsen in 1990, I walked into a bank to exchange my dollars for Czech crowns. I stopped cold when I noticed a poster depicting a couple of World War II American soldiers. Since the caption was in the Czech language, I didn't understand the purpose of the poster. As I was puzzling over it, someone approached me from behind. I felt a touch on my shoulder. When I turned around, I saw a tall, older gentleman, probably in his sixties, dressed in a suit that was partially covered by a dark trench coat. He also wore a black fedora. He must have realized that I was from the West because he spoke to me directly in English and politely asked, "May I help you?" I was so thrilled to hear my native tongue that I wanted to hug him. I had been interviewing Czechoslovakians through interpreters for about a week now, so the thought of being able to ask questions directly in English was very appealing to me.

Instead of hugging the older man, I politely asked him, "I was wondering what the caption on the poster says. Could you please translate it for me?" He explained, "It announces the opening of a new American Museum, located just down the street from the bank. The museum's purpose is to say thank you to the Armored Division of the United States Third Army for liberating the city of Pilsen at the end of World War II."

Still feeling enthralled at meeting a person who spoke English, I couldn't hold my excitement back anymore. It must have really shown because when I asked him, "May I buy you a cup of coffee?" He was taken aback. He exclaimed, "My, you are a very forward woman!" I immediately shrunk in embarrassment. With a nervous laugh, I explained why I was in Pilsen. As I calmed myself down, I asked him, "Could you please spare me some time to answer a few questions about the history of the city? Also, I would like to get specific directions to the museum." Before I could say more, he responded with a smile and said, "Come with me. I will buy *you* a cup of coffee." I sheepishly followed him.

After we left the bank, he escorted me to a small café, where we sat down at a small table. The café was not full, and the doors were open to the street since it was a nice, sunny day. As we sat down, I felt a cool breeze drape over me. It felt very refreshing since the bank's air had been tainted by strong body odor. Since locals only had hot water once a week, I imagined that very few would take a cold bath. After we sat down, my new companion ordered us some coffee, and I got ready to take some notes.

The distinguished-looking man told me that he was the Minister of Transportation of Czechoslovakia, hence his professional dress and demeanor. He had been educated in England before World War II, which explained why he spoke English so well. I then asked, "Who were the soldiers in the poster on the bank wall?" He explained, "They were members of the outfit that had liberated the city of Pilsen from the Nazis. One of those soldiers became my friend." He then told me his story.

The man was twenty years old when the U.S. army fought the battle at Pilsen Church that liberated the city. After the U.S. Army defeated the Nazis, a two-month occupation by the Americans occurred before the Soviet Union took control over Czechoslovakia. During the American occupation, he had become friends with the American soldier. He was hoping to see that same soldier again at a reunion, scheduled to be held in July 1990, a month after my visit.

The Minister of Transportation seemed very sincere when he told me that the American soldiers had been kind to his people. He said, "My people were very grateful to the Americans for providing much-needed food and medicine during the two-month occupation at the end of World War II. The kind treatment was such a contrast to the Nazis' brutal rule. Nazi soldiers had tortured and killed many people and not just the Jewish people that they especially targeted. They killed many non-Jewish as well. Rape was also a common occurrence."

As I listened to him, I had great sympathy for him. His country had been through so much brutality. I knew, though, that I could never fully understand the anguish and terror that had been inflicted on the Czechoslovakian people by the tyrannical powers that once ruled them.

After having coffee with the Minister of Transportation, he kindly escorted me to the newly formed American museum. At the time, the museum was located in a basement of one of the old buildings just down the street from the café and bank. It had only a couple of rooms, but it was filled with artifacts from the World War II era. After we walked down a few stairs and entered the museum, I noticed a musty smell like the odor of mothballs in my grandmother's closet.

The museum contained pictures of the U.S. Army liberating the city from the Nazi occupation. It also contained musical instruments, clothing, an American soldier's uniform, weapons, and other memorabilia that the people of Pilsen had hidden from the occupying communists after World War II. There was even displayed a baseball bat, ball, and glove, indicating that games were played when the U.S. Army was there.

My guide then explained the importance of these relics from World War II. "The communists tried to remove all traces of evidence that the U.S. army had even been in Pilsen. The people risked imprisonment or worse by hiding the memorabilia from the communists during the forty plus years of their occupation." It amazed me that the people remembered, after all those years, the two short months that the Americans were there. Then I saw a sign saying: *We will never forget you, boys.*

The Minister of Transportation said, "The communists were just as oppressive as the Nazis, and that they were rapists and murderers, too. The two months with the Americans were the best two months of my life." He then exclaimed, "It is easy to remember them!" I thought to myself, tyranny kills, but kindness, treating others as you want to be treated, brings optimism, and it is fondly remembered. It is the reason that I vividly remember my kind grandmother and my meeting with Fats Domino.

He explained further, "During the communist occupation, it was taught in the schools that the Soviet Army had liberated the whole country from the Nazis. The communists rewrote history in order to teach that they were the true heroes of World War II. All traces that other allied forces had ever been in the country were removed." Not only did communists push atheism on the people, but they also tried to rewrite history to suit their worldview. They used lies to glamorize communism.

Communist ideas alone could not win over hearts and minds. Lies had to be spun to prop up the worldview. Then the lies were forced on the people. The people lived with psychological torture, knowing that what they were force-fed was untrue and knowing that they would be imprisoned or killed if they did not accept the lies. Yet, at the same time, some had bravely saved the artifacts that I saw in the museum in spite of the known risk.

The last thing that the Minister of Transportation showed me was a small picture of a young man cutting off a Nazi flag from a major building in downtown Pilsen. The man in the picture was perched on an overhang of the building while cutting down the flag. As I looked at the picture, he asked me with a smile, "Who do you think that young man is?" Of course, I didn't know. But as I looked up at him and saw the gleam in his eyes, I felt a wave of electricity go through me. I exclaimed, "It was you!" With a humble nod, he smiled. Then, he told me that it was time for him to get on with his day.

After my tour of the museum, he went his way, and I went mine. As I walked back to my hotel, I wondered in amazement. I was so thankful to have accidentally met him. I wondered if it had been a divine appointment. Hearing his personal story and point of view helped me better understand what had taken place in the city of Pilsen. I noticed that when history has a personal story, it becomes much more interesting.

When I returned to Pilsen in 2019, I couldn't find the American museum that I had visited in 1990. Instead, I visited a newer museum called the Patton Memorial Pilsen Museum. I took my time going through the museum. It was much more organized and had much more information about the military events that had taken place in 1945. I tried to find the picture that I saw in 1990 of the young man cutting down the Nazi flag, but sadly, it wasn't there. However, the new museum had much to see, as described in its advertisement: "Decades have passed since that Sunday on the 6th of May 1945, when the 16th Armored Division on the Third United States Army under the command of General Patton entered Pilsen´s territory. In the days of May 1945, when the Allied forces had reached Czechoslovakia, the war came to an end not only for Pilsen but also for the whole Europe. Take a journey with us to the time of the liberation of Pilsen and Southwest Bohemia by the U.S. Army at our guided tour and the Patton Memorial Pilsen Museum. This memorial maps the liberation efforts of the U.S. Army in Pilsen and South-West Bohemia in 1945. You will see period footage, authentic photographs of the liberation, texts describing historical events, equipment and weaponry, personal items and memorabilia, etc."

In 2019, I visited the city square again in Pilsen. To my delight, there was a memorial to the American soldiers that had freed the city in 1945. The memorial had been erected in 1995 to commemorate the event and to thank the American soldiers who had liberated the city. It is called the *Thank You America Memorial*.[43] Not only is there a prominent statue located in the city square, but the people of Pilsen celebrate the anniversary of the liberation in May of every year. When I visited the memorial, I felt very proud of my country. I also remembered the man that I had met in 1990. He made a point to tell me that he was so thankful for America. I believe that he was most likely one of the people behind putting up the memorial.

Thank you America Memorial in Plisen

43 LRE Foundation, 2019

With all of the negative propaganda being spread today about the United States, it was so nice to hear positive stories about our military history. The Czechs did not consider America to be imperialistic. The United States is remembered as a liberator. Not only did the American military liberate and aid the people of Pilsen at the end of World War II, they never imposed any type of colonial rule. The communists were the ones guilty of imperialism. A verse came to mind when I mulled over the contrast, Proverbs 29:2, "When the righteous thrive, the people rejoice; when the wicked rule, the people groan."

In 1990, the people in Pilsen were in a festive mood. After meeting with the Minister of Transportation, I returned to the hotel. Then, I joined the tour group for dinner. We ate at a pub, and even though there was a feeling of celebration in the city air, no locals were eating out with us. I didn't get to question anyone else during our stay, but I was so thankful to have met the Minister of Transportation.

I left the city of Pilsen, understanding that the Czechs had good memories of America but bad memories of both the Nazi and communist rules. I am not sure that the Slovakians had that same experience.

Even though both the Czechs and the Slovakians wanted independence from the Soviet Union, the Slovakians also wanted freedom from the Czechs. Some Slovakians even hung on to the values of communism. The overall ideology seemed to be more atheistic than the Czechs. Amazingly, I would soon meet a Slovakian who would help explain these observations.

Bratislava

June 1990, Bratislava, Czechoslovakia

Another stop on the tour was Bratislava, the largest and the capital city of Slovakia. It is over one thousand years old and is located on the Danube River. The oldest structure is Bratislava Castle, which dates back to the tenth century. However, the castle hill area has been settled since the Bronze age.[44] We only spent one day in Bratislava, though, so I didn't get a chance to visit any tourist sites.

In 1990, the mood in Bratislava was far different than the mood in Prague. The people seemed much more subdued. It was also a dreary day, as the sun barely peaked out from behind the clouds. Political party posters were plastered all over the city, encouraging the people to vote for candidates of different political parties. Anti-communist posters were among the other posters. One poster read *Stop Communism* and was printed next to a hand placed over a red star. The hammer and sickle symbol of communism had already been chipped out of the concrete buildings. This action was happening all throughout Czechoslovakia.

44 Wikipedia, 2021

I didn't meet anyone in Bratislava to interview. From my observations in the city, plus the lower-keyed atmosphere in Slovakia, I sensed that something was different here. The people did not seem very excited about the new republic. The social changes that I observed in Bohemia were not apparent in Slovakia.

As I was puzzling over the obvious differences between Bohemia and Slovakia, the tour group made a stop for lunch. After we disembarked from our bus, we entered a fairly large restaurant with many empty tables. It was a clean, modern-looking building, with a long bar that we passed by as we walked in to find a table. We were the only customers in the restaurant.

As we chose a table, I could see waiters, mostly young men in dark suits, standing and conversing with each other at the bar. I assumed that we would be served quickly, but I was wrong. It took twenty minutes to finally be served. As we sat waiting, we all became very perplexed, and a bit irritated, wondering why we were being ignored. Finally, a waiter walked over to our table. As our tour guide gave him our order in the Czech language, I sensed a coldness in the waiter. I did not feel welcome. When we left the restaurant, I was happy that we would not be spending much time in the city.

The experience in the restaurant reinforced my ideas about communism. I came to the conclusion that the coldness in the workers wasn't personal. Since workers, including the restaurant attendants, receive the same amount of pay whether they work or not, there is little motivation to provide good service. I do not believe that many people in Bratislava had the money to spend on restaurants, so I think that the waiters were surprised that there was work to do on that day.

The next day, we traveled to another Slovakian town called Trnava. I was not unhappy about leaving Bratislava. I knew depression very well personally, and if I could call any city depressed, it would be Bratislava.

Trnava

June 1990, Trnava, Czechoslovakia

Trnava is the oldest town and the industrial center of western Slovakia. It is known as a walled city and has the nickname Little Rome[45] since it has a large number of Catholic churches. The largest is St. John the Baptist Cathedral, which has two steeples. The cathedral is of Baroque style and was built in 1629. It is part of a complex of academic buildings and is not used for spiritual purposes.[46]

As we drove into the city, I noticed the steeples, but I also noticed some disrepair in the buildings. There were bricks peeking out from behind the stucco faces of some of the buildings. The town was mostly empty of pedestrians and cars, but it was a very impressive looking city due to its old architecture. The Renaissance-style Town Tower in Trinity Square was built in 1574. It is eight stories high and contains a Baroque-style copula holding a gilded statue of the Virgin Mary. The tower clockwork was constructed in 1729, and the bells chime - every quarter of an hour.[47]

---

45 Wikipedia, 2021
46 Id.
47 Trnava.sk, 2021

I was told that the tower was used as a lookout during the Middle Ages.

Disrepair in buildings

The city has a strong history of ideological clashes and religious fanaticism. This was the site of a clash between the Hussites of the Protestant movement and the Hapsburgs of the Catholic church during the Middle Ages. It is a town that has also had its share of tyrannical control.

The Hussite movement had begun in Bohemia and eventually spread throughout Czechoslovakia. It was the most important forerunner of the Protestant Reformation. The religious movement was ignited by social issues stemming from the tyranny of the Roman Catholic church leadership during this time. The church had executed the leader of the early Hussites, Jan Hus, for heresy in July of 1415. He was a theologian at Charles University who spoke out against the selling of indulgences for the forgiveness of sins by the Catholic church.[48] For a number of years afterward, wars between the Hussites and the Catholics continued. Those wars helped strengthen Czech nationalism.

I had been told that the Jesuit University had previously existed in Trnava until the communist takeover in 1948. It was alleged that the monastery was gutted and then converted to barracks for communist soldiers. Supposedly, many priests were either killed or imprisoned by the communist government. This action was greatly resented and never forgotten by the people in the town. However, I can find no information to back up this claim now.

Anti-Semitism also existed in Trnava even before the Nazis came to power. For example, I learned that it was local people who had destroyed the Jewish temple in town prior to World War II. It was never rebuilt.

---

48 Wikipedia, 2021

In 1990, the ideological attitude of the majority of the people was much less religious in scope than in previous centuries. I learned that a large Hussite church had seen a resurgence in attendance, but the main concern of the people was politics.

The Slovak National party had captured many votes in the initial election after the Velvet Revolution. The party's ideology was originally based on European Christian values, but that had changed under communism. It is also the oldest party in Slovakia. The party brokered Slovakia's independence from Bohemia in 1993.[49] The Slovakians wanted to have a distinct identity from the Czechs.

Even though the Slovakian people wanted democracy, it was interesting to note that very few changes had been made in their local leadership. I was astonished to learn later that many of the leaders in Slovakia were former communists. The ideology of communism still existed underneath the veneer of revolution and independence. Eventually, on January 1, 1993, Slovakia became independent from the newly formed Czech Republic. Like the Velvet Revolution, the dissolution of Czechoslovakia was peaceful. It is humorously called the Velvet Divorce.[50]

---

49 Wikipedia, 2021
50 Id.

As I walked through Trinity Square, the main square in Trnava, I heard the story of the town's statue, The Holy Trinity. Since it was a hot, sunny day, the heat was affecting my concentration as I tried to listen to our professor as he guided us through the square. In spite of the heat, I learned that the statue was built in 1695 and went missing in 1949 after the communists took control of the city.

The professor showed us a picture of the statue and described it for us. He explained, "The Holy Trinity features the Crowning of Mary at the top of the statue. On its base sit four saints, St. Anthony of Padua, Saint Florian, Agatha of Sicily, and Francis Xavier." He then added, "The communists did not want this religious statue to be in prominent display in the city, so they took it down." I felt sad that I didn't get to see it. The square seemed somewhat bare without it. I was glad when I heard afterward that the government had promised to return the statue to the people and to the square again soon.

In 1990, I was told that a petition had been made to the state to return the Jesuit University property back to the people. They did not want the state to use it anymore for soldiers' quarters. Even though the people were not very religious as a whole, they were appalled at the desecration of the monastery and the other religious symbols in their city. The majority of the people wanted to preserve their religious history.

When we left the city of Trnava, even though I did not meet any locals, I admired the tenaciousness of the people. They had held on to their traditions and history. Although the people of Trnava were not religious, they still rejected Soviet rule. They also rejected Czech rule. An independent spirit remained. I began to wonder again about the reason for the difference in the attitudes between the Czechs and Slovaks. I had yet to meet a man who would explain this difference to me.

Hlohovec

June 1990, Hlohovec, Czechoslovakia

The last city in Czechoslovakia that we visited was the industrial city of Hlohovec, located in western Slovakia. It has a population of about twenty-one thousand people.[51] As we drove into the city, I noticed how drab some of the buildings appeared. Many people lived in concrete apartment buildings without siding or paint. Those buildings were built during communist rule. Again, I noticed disrepair and a lack of color in the city. I did notice nice furnishings inside the two apartments that I visited, but the wallpaper appeared to be from an older era.

In this city, Slovakian ideology became more understandable to me. Upon fortuitously meeting a middle-aged man who spoke English, I hired him to be my interpreter for the three-day visit. He was of medium height and medium build. He had longish, dark brown hair and brown eyes. I was very excited to be able to interview him, along with some other important people in the city. My interpreter set up meetings for me

51 Wikipedia, 2021

to meet the mayor, a wire factory president, and its manager. I also met a student and a soldier.

Since my interpreter spoke English very well, I wanted to know how he had learned the language. I asked him, "How did you learn to speak English?" He said, "My Canadian aunt sent me some Johnny Cash records, and I listened to BBC when I could." I was so impressed that he learned the language using only those two mediums.

He was an artist and painted propaganda billboards and did drawings for cartoons in the city's newspaper for the Communist Party. After he showed me some of his work, I expressed admiration for his talent. Then, I pulled out from my large bag a daily newspaper that I had brought with me from Minnesota. He was astonished when he saw that it was printed every day. His city's newspaper only came out once a month.

The interpreter and his wife also worked at the local wire factory. His attractive wife had short, blondish hair. She was also very kind. Their daughters were both grown, so he and his wife lived alone together in their apartment. He was ashamed to tell me that he had bribed an official to get one of his daughters into college, but he was very proud that he had never joined the Communist Party. Through this man, I got a deeper look at life in Slovakia.

I also enjoyed his wit. He agreed with me that humor was very important in life. The delivery of one of his sayings greatly amused me. He said with a serious look, "The town square is very important in Slovakian life. There is a pub on one corner to get drunk. On another corner, there is a clinic to get sober. Finally, on another corner, there is a church to repent." With a pause, he quipped, "Then, you do it all over again."

The Interviews

My first appointment with my new friend and interpreter was with the mayor of Hlohovec. The mayor was a distinguished, slightly greying man. He had a stiff demeanor when I interviewed him. He noticeably pulled back when I asked him some political questions. Through my interpreter, I asked him if he was looking forward to more open relations with the West. He responded cautiously, "We open the door slowly. We do not want to get blown out in the draft." He then said, "Havel has made some mistakes. He sent bankers, police, teachers, customs officers, and state employees in from Bohemia. This makes the Slovakians very nervous. We think that the Czechs are trying to misuse us economically. For example, they take our raw materials for production. We have a saying that goes like this, 'Cows that graze here, should be milked here.'"

When I asked the mayor about education in Slovakia, he grudgingly complained, "The Czechs have a better opportunity to be educated. All ministries of foreign trade are centered in Prague, and the people there will have much more opportunities to work abroad and learn other languages. However, Slovakians are more diligent than the Czechs; the Czechs just want a bigger piece of the pie!" Since I am quoting him through my translator, I may not have gotten every word correctly, but the resentment that I heard in the mayor's voice did not need translation.

From my observations, I wasn't really sold on the idea that the Slovakians were more diligent than the Czechs, but certainly, they were more cautious about the new government. Some Slovakians believed that they were being treated like lower-class citizens. It reminded me of the strained race relations that we have had in America. The Czechs did not mention having resentment toward the Slovakians. They only mentioned resentment toward the communists. It did appear to me that the Czechs, in general, were more ambitious and possibly unaware or unconcerned about the plight of the Slovakians.

The next person that I interviewed was a manager of a wire factory. He told me through my interpreter that some people were afraid of sinking living standards. Even though he admitted that communism should fall, he thought that life was freer and easier under communism.

I learned later that the manager had also been one of the communist elites. He thought that since people could take whatever they wanted from the factories without any questions, they could also live better, even with the existing low salaries. I was told by my interpreter that the boss stole more than anyone else, setting the example for the others to follow. The wire factory manager also acknowledged that it was good that people were freer to express their thoughts, but he didn't like it that people couldn't continue the practice of taking whatever they wanted at the factory. His last statement to me was, "I don't care who is in government, I just want a full glass of wine!" I appreciated his honesty, and I think that a lot of people all over the world think the same way.

As I thought later about the conversation with the factory manager, I agreed that people do want their needs met. I also believe that freedom is important. It does matter who has power. Even in America, people running for office make promises, but they do not sometimes fulfill their promises when elected. Some are not sincere in their promises and will lie just to get elected. Others may be sincere, but they are unable to fulfill the promises due to failures in leadership or because the promises are impossibilities. The work to accomplish the promise may be too great, or the obstacles in the way may be too big. The freedom for the electorate to evaluate and choose the politicians that they trust is therefore very valuable. If the politicians do not do the job as promised, they can be kicked out of office in the next election. This can only happen in a free and fair election.

Besides the loss of freedom under communism, the system also created a negative economic impact. There was no abundance of goods in communist Czechoslovakia. Stores had the basics, but there were very few stores and very few choices, even in groceries. I also have no example of a communist system that has provided wealth and well-being for its people. Some people claim that Sweden is an example of a socialist system that works. However, Sweden's economic system is mainly capitalistic. The state does not own the means of production in Sweden. Instead, through high taxes, their system has created a social network for those who have a sub-standard income. Sweden's wealth is created by a capitalist system, even though it redistributes a significant portion of that wealth to its poorer citizens.

I then spent time with the daughter of the manager that I had just interviewed. She spoke some English, so we communicated with each other the best that we could. She took me on a short bus tour of the city while telling me a little bit about her life. At home on break from attending Charles University in Prague, she was looking forward to her future after school. She had aspirations to become an engineer. She did not seem to have any serious political views.

As we tried to talk about her university experience, the manager's daughter nonchalantly revealed to me that she would cheat on exams. I was truly shocked by her lack of conscience. I think that she picked up on what I was thinking by the look of shock on my face and said in halting English, "You like mom. I love mom, but she Catholic." When I told her that I believed in God, she responded, "All I need is my good."

Afterward, when I evaluated her philosophy, I realized that one of the outcomes of atheism is the idea that "whatever is good for me, is good." There is no need to consider the welfare of others. In Christianity, the Golden Rule is one of the main teachings, *treat others as you want to be treated*. Communists, who are atheists, believe that all moral authority comes from government, since to them, there exists no higher power. The state, collectivism, and materialism are valued in communism. Christianity teaches concern for others and emphasizes the value of the individual. Since the two ideologies are not compatible and almost opposite from one another, it made sense that the communists banned religion. It also made sense that the conflict of ideologies caused a rift in this young student's family.

Next, I met the student's boyfriend. He was a young man in officers' training for the army. He was not very friendly to me, but I tried to talk to him anyway. He could speak English. After I was introduced to him, he looked at me with disdain and said, "Americans are too outspoken." Even though I had to somewhat agree that Americans can come across as brash or forward like I was with the Minister of Transportation, I responded, "Americans highly value free speech, which is why we are not afraid to speak our thoughts." He thought that it was too dangerous to allow free speech, but he didn't tell me why. He also told me that Americans are too interested in war. He failed to see that communist aggression was also a cause for war.

The boyfriend had accepted the communist propaganda that America is evil, and he wasn't going to change his mind. I responded that Americans do not like war. I explained, "For example, in the late 1980s, there were protests about the U.S. arms-buildup under Ronald Reagan." He responded, "That may be true, but your government still likes war."

I did not say anything else, even though I would have liked to have said to him that the Reagan doctrine promoted peace through strength and did not promote war. I understood that many people believe that the build-up of arms is saber-rattling; therefore, I sensed that it would be futile to argue further with this soldier. I strongly felt his suspiciousness of me, so I ended the conversation. A creepy feeling came over me while I was talking to him. I was starting to feel like I was being viewed as an international spy. I also realized that not all people in Eastern Europe were freedom-loving. Some still held onto communist ideology.

I had a very brief interview with the wire factory president. Early in the interview, I mistakenly asked him if he had been a member of the Communist Party. My interpreter gave me a strange, frightened, and quizzical look while asking me if I really wanted to ask the question. I answered, "Yes, please." Later, I regretted asking the question. I didn't fully understand the danger that it could impose on my interpreter.

Instead of answering my question, the president abruptly got up and left the room. When we left the factory, my interpreter explained that it was very dangerous for me to ask that question. The president did not want to confess openly that he had been a member of the Communist Party because he feared that he could lose his job or, worse, under the new democratic republic. I felt again an uneasy feeling that I might have been viewed as an international spy. I also realized that just as those wanting freedom feared another communist takeover, communists feared retribution from the new government.

The Retired Nurse

During my visit in Hlohovec, I spent the three nights in an apartment with a retired nurse. I took very quick, cold baths each morning due to the lack of hot water. Hot water was only available once a week for the locals. I remember kneeling in a deep, old-fashioned cast-iron tub, shivering while splashing the very cold water over my body and bending my head under the faucet to wash my hair. It was an unforgettable experience.

The apartment had a small refrigerator but no freezer. The refrigerator looked similar to one that my grandmother had in the 1950s. It was basically a small icebox. The feather bed was very comfortable, and I wished that I could have brought it home with me. I had a very good night's sleep in it.

When I first arrived at her apartment, she welcomed me by smiling and expressing a welcome in the Czech language. She went to the cupboard in the kitchen and pulled out a glass, signifying that she was offering me something to drink. I nodded a grateful yes. Instead of reaching into the small refrigerator as I expected, she went into her pantry and brought back a warm bottle of grape soda. After opening the drink, she poured some into the glass and handed it to me. I took a couple of sips, realizing that I did not care for warm grape soda, but I was thankful to have something to drink. I then sat down at her kitchen table, trying to think of a way to communicate with her.

Since the nurse did not speak any English, it was hard to question her about her experiences living under communism. We tried to use my German dictionary to communicate. For that reason, I limited my questions to be about health care in the country. She responded with a thumbs down when I asked about health care. As frustrating as our communication was to both of us, I managed to get the following information: 1) The communist system created long queues to see a doctor; 2) If a person needed surgery, he or she had to pay extra under the table; and 3) Some had died waiting for an operation. Even in healthcare, the black market was alive and well. People had to use the illegal system to get needed surgeries as well as other needed items.

I appreciated the nurse's hospitality, but I did not spend much time with her. I spent most of my time with my new friend, the interpreter.

Evening with the Interpreter

During my last night in Hlohovec, I was invited to dinner at my interpreter's home. I happily accepted.

Since he spoke English so well, it was a treat to spend the whole evening with him. His wife was very sweet, but she didn't speak English, so I didn't direct very many questions to her. She served me a wonderful meal, including freshly baked bread, a chicken dish which included bits of potato, and a plate of numerous types of sliced cheeses. It smelled as delicious as it tasted. And I wondered if she spent more on the meal than she normally would. I made the mistake of calling her a peach. I have no idea why I used that word to describe her since I do not normally relate people to peaches, but it was meant to be a compliment. My interpreter laughed out loud and said, "You just called my wife a loose woman!" After we all had a good laugh, he said, "Do not bring us white roses either, because white roses signify death."

As the night went on, the conversation became more serious. I asked him why the Slovakians were so different from the Bohemians. He was able to give me some interesting insights into the people that I had met in Hlohovec. I asked, "Why were some unhappy about the coming democracy in the country?" He explained, "First of all, the mayor and president of the factory are both ex-communists. They had both turned in their Communist Party memberships and joined the Slovak National Party." That explained their coldness and unwillingness to talk politics with me. The men both knew that the new government under Vaclav Havel could have them arrested since they were former communist leaders. Therefore, they were very hesitant to talk to me. I was also an American, and America was still their enemy.

The average Slovakian was afraid of the Soviet Union. They believed that the hard-liners of the Communist Party, like the factory president and the mayor of Hlohovec, could regain authoritarian power again. My interpreter told me next, "The new nationalistic party is just a cover-up for the true purposes of the communists. If the party can succeed in separating the Slovakians from the Bohemians, then they can quickly go back to doing things as before. The communist leadership can then regain control." Then he said, "I do not dislike the Czechs. I have some friends that live in Bohemia."

He expressed his admiration for Vaclav Havel and said that he cried when the new president gave his first address over television. He explained, "I love my country, and I am proud that we are our own country again." I believed him when he said that he was afraid of the Communist Party. I also realized then how very brave he was to be my interpreter, as he could suffer a lot because of me if the communists regained control. As the realization sunk in, I felt very bad that I had asked the president of the factory if he was a communist. A return to communism would not be good for my interpreter and his wife.

Because English had been a banned language before the Velvet Revolution, no one had known, except for the interpreter's wife, that he could speak English. He was so happy to finally be able to use his language skills. He had been just as excited to meet me as I was to meet him. I was the first American that he had met, and I was the first person who had hired him to be an interpreter. I felt honored.

The interpreter also told me what life was like for women in his country. Many of the factory workers were women. They did heavy lifting, operated heavy machinery, and did other types of labor.

I shared that I was taught in my college classes that the communist system was much more equitable toward women than the American capitalist system. From what I witnessed in my tour of the factory, though, that did not appear to be true. Men had management roles, and the women did the actual work. My interpreter agreed that men got better jobs. On top of that, after work, women were expected to wait in line to do the shopping, do all the cleaning and cooking, and care for the children.

Waiting in line to shop was not fun for the locals. The stores did not allow more than one customer in them at a time. The people would stand in a queue outside of the store and wait for a store attendant to let them in. The first time that I made an attempt to enter a store, I didn't notice the short line, and I tried to enter as I would in the United States. I was angrily shooed away. I didn't understand my mistake until I turned around and saw the women waiting behind me. Feeling embarrassed and a little rattled from the scolding, I went to stand at the back of the line.

Thinking about the burden that the women carried in Slovakia, I asked my interpreter, "What do men do after work?" He laughingly said, "We are lazy. We watch the football game on television." I smiled and said, "It's no different in the United States." But then he sheepishly said, "I do help my wife sometimes." I knowingly smiled at his wife, even though she did not understand what her husband had just said.

He said that there were other reasons that some of the people were dissatisfied with the communist system. The environment was suffering, and nothing much was being done about it. He remembers fishing as a boy in the river but sadly stated that it was now too polluted to do any fishing. Since there were no pollution controls, factories dumped waste directly into the river. Another issue in the city was the nuclear power plant built by the Soviets. A fear existed that a nuclear accident could happen as the 1989 event in Chernobyl, Russia. Distrust in the competency of Russian engineering was very high.

Most of the people in Slovakia believed that the Soviets had exploited them. My interpreter cited one example, "We supplied all the raw material and labor to build the pipeline into the Soviet Union for all our oil needs. They rewarded us by charging us twice the amount that the rest of the world pays for oil! The Bohemians would never exploit us like that."

After a wonderful evening, I had some insight into the life of a Slovakian. Not all Slovakians were atheists, and not all were communists, even though many still were. Hard-line communists seemed much more interested in self-promotion and self-gratification. Those leaning towards freedom seemed more interested in the well-being of society and, surprisingly, seemed more interested in protecting the environment.

About six months after my visit to Czechoslovakia in January of 1991, the interpreter from Hlohovec came to Minnesota to visit me. When I picked him up at the airport, we were experiencing blizzard-like conditions. He exclaimed as we stepped outside to go to our car, "Oh no! Am I in Siberia?" We all had a laugh. The first time that I took him to one of our grocery stores, he seemed to go into shock again. He fell to his knees, saying, "Am I in heaven?" He couldn't believe all the fresh fruits and vegetables that were available in our little grocery store in the middle of the winter. I also smiled when he told me that I work too hard. He certainly didn't understand capitalism. Just as I had experienced when I first got to Czechoslovakia, he was experiencing culture shock in Minnesota.

A Comparison of the Economies Between 1990 and 2019

Upon returning to the Czech Republic in September of 2019, almost thirty years after my first visit, I saw the effect that freedom had on the country. The country was much more prosperous. I saw evidence all around me that the people are experiencing better livelihoods. Houses were being built, repaired, and painted. Cars were plentiful, and small businesses were flourishing. Modern conveniences were the norm. The tourist business had greatly increased. When I first crossed the Charles bridge in 1990, I was almost alone, as there was little pedestrian traffic. In 2019, because of the crowds, it was hard to avoid bumping into people.

Crowds on Charles Bridge in 2019

In a free economy, the individual has an opportunity to invest owned resources and use his or her talents to create as much personal wealth as possible. Under communism, there is no personal choice or investment. There is no satisfaction from pursuing an occupation of choice. I saw a huge difference when I compared the stagnant economy of 1990 with the prosperous economy of 2019.

When people are free to create their own wealth, they can then also contribute more to their community. Free, prosperous people tend to be givers. Being able to earn a good living from an occupation of choice creates benevolence. The United States is the most giving country in the world, and I don't think that is by accident. In spite of the country's imperfections, it has also been the freest and prosperous country in the world. It is the reason that people all over the world want to live there.

The government does not know each individual's capabilities and aspirations, and therefore, cannot choose wisely for another individual's occupation. In 1990, I heard other stories about people being forced to change professions. Besides the story of the carpenter being forced to become a bus driver in Chynice, another story involved a surgeon being forced to become a locksmith. One day, when changing locks for an elite politician, the politician asked him why it was taking him so long to do the job. The surgeon sarcastically responded, "I was trained to be a surgeon and not a locksmith." He was not in an occupation that was using his skillsets well. The government had wasted the surgeon's education by making him be a locksmith.

Healthy, competent people desire to be valued individuals within society. They want just compensation for their accomplishments. If one person gives their all to improve society, for example, studies to become a great surgeon, but another one only wants to live off of society without contributing to it, why should each get the same reward? A society that only wants equality of outcome punishes achievers and rewards the lazy. It discourages the creation of wealth and encourages unproductivity. Since a prosperous nation can provide more assistance to those citizens that cannot provide for themselves, it makes logical sense to encourage people to be as productive as possible.

Meaningful work was a goal of communism, but it was not apparent to me at all in 1990 that this was true in the lives of the people that I met. Under communism, many people do not always work, even if they have a job. During my stay, I visited a state farm and a cooperative farm. The state farm was for growing food on a much larger scale than the cooperative farm, which mainly grew vegetables for the neighborhood in which it was found. I found more people working in the cooperative farm than I found working in the state farm. I believe that it was mainly because the cooperative farmworkers benefited more directly from their labors. In the cooperative farm, the vegetables grown would eventually be on that same worker's table.

People working in a Cooperative Farm

The state farm that I visited in 1990 was almost devoid of workers, and there was a tractor stuck in a drying, muddy rut. I asked the man who was giving me the tour, "Why is that tractor stuck in the mud?" He said with a chuckle, "Because the government had planned ahead of time the date to plant, but they couldn't control the weather." Ironically, if the workers had not tried to plant on that day, they would have been in trouble with the government. The planning autocrats did not understand the basics of farming. An experienced farmer, or any sane individual, knows that you do not try to plant seed into a rainy, muddy field. An experienced farmer waits for the first dry day in the planting season to plow a field.

Even though it was sunny on the day that I visited the state farm, no one was working in the field. No one was planting or even trying to free the tractor that was stuck in the mud. In a similar situation at my childhood farm, I know that my dad would have been in the field working to free a stuck tractor. Even so, I don't remember a tractor getting stuck in any field at my childhood farm.

The people that have knowledge of their professions should also be the people to make decisions about their particular businesses. Autocrats do not have the boots-on-the-ground understanding of what is happening in the various businesses and cannot make immediate decisions to run the economy efficiently and for the benefit of society. After forty-plus years of a planned economy, it is amusing to me that the communist elite hadn't learned a thing about farming. You would assume that they would have at least realized that tractors do get stuck in the mud on rainy days and would have adjusted their plans accordingly.

The black market also existed extensively to compensate for scarcities in 1990. If a person needed surgery but was not scheduled in time to save his or her life, he or she could pay the surgeon under the table to bump them up in the patient queue. One of the problems of socialized medicine is the long wait times. The doctors get paid the same wage whether ten or fifty patients are served. Of course, most doctors chose to see a lesser number of patients.

Other forms of the black market existed as well in 1990. I was warned not to sell on the street anything of value, for example, my jeans or my dollars, or I could go to jail. In spite of the threat of jail, the black market still existed and thrived beneath the nose of the communist government. In 2019, I was not warned about the black market like I was in 1990. Maybe it had gone deeper underground, but I was not aware of its existence in 2019. I also believe that there wasn't a great need for it in the robust capitalistic environment.

Going Home

As I left Czechoslovakia at the end of June in 1990, my passport received a mark with the date that I left the newly founded Czech and Slovak Federative Republic. When I had first entered the country, it had been stamped with a Czechoslovakian Socialist Republic passport mark. I was so excited to be going home, as I really missed my children and my language. I had experienced much in just a short time. The trip was a defining point in my life. I didn't just learn about communism. I learned so much about myself.

The most important thing that I learned wasn't about how communism affected the economy of Czechoslovakia. I learned that the value of the individual is the most important aspect of society. Without freedom, an individual cannot fulfill his or her destiny. Without freedom of thought, an individual cannot search for truth. Without the ability to search for truth, there is no meaning in life. Without meaning in life, there is no dignity or purpose. Without dignity and purpose, there is no happiness. The pursuit of happiness is an inalienable right endowed by our Creator according to the United States Constitution. The spirit of tyranny's purpose is to take away that right. It attacks the individuals within society by enticing or forcing them to believe and act on lies. When individuals are not valued in a society, they become unproductive and feel worthless. Individual dignity is destroyed under tyranny's control. In controlling people, tyranny destroys potential achievements by them and eventually destroys prosperity and a healthy society.

When I arrived in New York after the first leg of my journey home, I wanted to kiss the ground. I was so relieved to be back in the United States and away from the constant tension that I had felt in Czechoslovakia. When I actually got home, I was exhausted but so happy to see my children again.

After I went back to my usual routine, I realized that I had changed. I no longer took for granted my freedoms. I had a newly found confidence in my abilities. I received an A on my term paper. My professor even asked me if he could put it into his library.

Out of the many things that I learned on my trip to Czechoslovakia, one thing stood out to me. I had to face the tyranny in my own life. I needed to acknowledge my value as a human being and stop listening to all those voices that had belittled me and controlled me. I found out that I could be free to become the person that God intended me to be. At the same time, I needed to face and forgive the people who had hurt me.

One of the last things Jesus is recorded to have said before he died on the cross is in Luke 23:24, "Father, forgive them, for they know not what they are doing." The spirit of tyranny loves to inhabit the lives of those who do not confront the evil in their life. Those people tend to be bitter and unforgiving. This verse helped me to understand that some of the people in my life did not realize the hurt that they had caused me. Or, even if they did, they may have thought that their actions were just. Forgiving is not an easy thing to do, but it is possible with God's help, and it is very beneficial. Forgiveness stops the abused from becoming abusers. It stops them from becoming new faces of tyranny.

In 1992, two years after my trip, I left my unhappy marriage and filed for legal separation. I was still hoping that we could reconcile. Then, after a year of being separated, I dropped the legal separation due to differences in the law between Minnesota and my new state of residence. My husband's lawyer then filed for divorce.

Even though I had tried to right any of my perceived wrongs in our marriage, my husband and I were not on the same wavelength. I still did not feel respected or loved, and I could no longer live in an environment that did not value me as a person. The years of resentment and misunderstandings between us had taken their toll.

My faith would be tested many times in my life in the years to come. I would not always have victory. I am not a perfect person. I have not always done the right things or made the right decisions. I have not been a perfect mother either, as my children can attest. However, I have tried to make amends with those that I have hurt and confront and make peace with those who have hurt me. Romans 12:18 says, "if it is possible, as much as it is up to you, be at peace with all people." Sadly, it is not always possible to be at peace with others who disagree with you or don't value you, and in those cases, the relationship usually ends.

It has taken me many more years to feel confident in my battle against tyranny, but I know that confi-

dence was birthed in me during my trip to Czechoslovakia in 1990. I learned that truth, faith, and courage
are the main weapons to use in facing tyranny. Life
is a journey, and I want to make the most of it! I still
want to be as brave as some of those people that I met
during my incredible trip to Czechoslovakia. I hope
you do, too!

Epilogue

Quoted below are verses from the New International Version of the Bible, which I believe sum up the battle that rages every day between evil and good - tyranny and freedom.

Ephesians 6:12: "For our struggle is not against flesh and blood, but against the rulers, against the authorities, against the powers of this dark world and against the spiritual forces of evil in the heavenly realms."

Ephesians 2:1: "As for you, you were dead in your transgressions and sins, in which you used to live when you followed the ways of this world and of the ruler of the kingdom of the air, the spirit who is now at work in those who are disobedient."

In John 10:10, Jesus is quoted by John as saying, "The thief comes to steal, kill and destroy. I have come that they may have life, and have it to the full."

I believe that one of the rulers amongst the spiritual forces of evil is tyranny. As a thief, its goal is to kill, steal and destroy the lives of people and society. The amazing thing is that we can choose good by choosing God. We do not need to be overcome by the dark forces. It is a struggle, as we do not live in a world free of evil, and no individual always chooses to do what is right and good. However, the value of each individual is enormous. A person who chooses good and feels valued can become a productive and benevolent part of society.

It is my belief that each individual needs to be valued and have the freedom to pursue his or her God-given right to pursue happiness within a fair and just society. The battle against tyranny will be one that needs to be fought every day. With truth, faith and courage, it can be defeated.

Bibliography

Bing. "Dictionary." Accessed June 30, 2021, https://www.bing.com/search?q=tyranny&form=PRUSEN&pc=EUPP_UF01&mkt=en-us&httpsmsn=1&msnews=1&rec_search=1&refig=cc056ef02ce9434b95a7f2c9f2c0ce66&sp=-1&ghc=1&pq=tyranny&sc=8-7&qs=n&sk=&cvid=cc056ef02ce9434b95a7f2c9f2c0ce66.

Braun, Janice, Conscience, and Captivity: Religion in Eastern Europe. Washington DC: Ethics and Public Policy Center; Lanham, Md., 1998.

Information Centre Karlovy Vary. "Peter's Height Lookout." Accessed August 2, 2021, https://www.karlovyvary.cz/en/peters-height-lookout.

LRE Foundation. "Europe Remembers." Accessed August 2, 2021, https://europeremembers.com/destination/thank-you-america-memorial/.

Prague Castle for Visitors. "Old Royal Palace." Accessed August 1, 2021, https://www.hrad.cz/en/prague-castle-for-visitors/objects-for-visitors/old-royal-palace-10332.

Michael Savage. "Michael Savage: Stalin's Head of Secret Police: 'Show Me the Man and I Will Show You The Crime.'" Accessed June 30, 2021, https://michaelsavage.com/stalins-head-of-secret-police-show-me-the-man-and-i-will-show-you-the-crime/.

The Getty Conservation Institute. "Conservation of the ST. Vitus Mosaic in Prague." Accessed August 1, 2021, https://www.getty.edu/conservation/our_projects/field_projects/vitus/.

Trnava.sk. "Basic information—City of Trnava." Accessed August 2, 2021, https://www.trnava.sk/en/article/historical-monuments.

University of Central Arkansas. "Czechoslovakia (1918-1992)." Accessed August 1, 2021, https://uca.edu/politicalscience/dadm-project/europerussiacentral-asia-region/czechoslovakia-1918-1992/.

Wikipedia. "1990 Czechiskivak presidential election." Accessed August 1, 2021, https://en.wikipedia.org/wiki/1990_Czechoslovak_presidential_election.

"Bratislava." Accessed August 2, 2021, https://en.wikipedia.org/wiki/Bratislava.

"Charles Bridge." Accessed August 1, 2021, https://en.wikipedia.org/wiki/Charles_Bridge.

"Czechoslovakia." Accessed July 31, 2021, https://en.wikipedia.org/wiki/Czechoslovakia.

"Dissolution of Czechoslovakia." Accessed August 2, 2021, https://en.wikipedia.org/wiki/Dissolution_of_Czechoslovakia.

"Doctor Zhivago." Accessed June 30, 2021, https://en.wikipedia.org/wiki/Doctor_Zhivago_(film).

"Eastern Bloc." Accessed June 30, 2021, https://en.wikipedia.org/wiki/Eastern_Bloc.

"Great Purge." Accessed June 30, 2021, https://en.wikipedia.org/wiki/Great_Purge.

"Gustáv Husák." Accessed August 1, 2021, https://en.wikipedia.org/wiki/Gust%C3%A1v_Hus%C3%A1k.

"Hlohovec." Accessed August 2, 2021, https://en.wikipedia.org/wiki/Hlohovec.

"Jan Hus." Accessed August 2, 2021, https://en.wikipedia.org/wiki/Jan_Hus.

"Jan Opletal." Accessed August 1, 2021, https://en.wikipedia.org/wiki/Jan_Opletal.

"Jewish Bolshevism." Accessed June 30, 2021,

https://en.wikipedia.org/wiki/Jewish_Bolshevism.

"Karlovy Vary." Accessed 8 02, 2021, https://en.wikipedia.org/wiki/Karlovy_Vary.

"Maria Theresa." Accessed June 30, 2021, https://en.wikipedia.org/wiki/Maria_Theresa.

"Mozarthaus Vienna." Accessed June 30, 2021, https://en.wikipedia.org/wiki/Mozarthaus_Vienna.

"Neville Chamberlain." Accessed June 20, 2021, https://en.wikipedia.org/wiki/Neville_Chamberlain.

"Plzeň." Accessed August 2, 2021, https://en.wikipedia.org/wiki/Plze%C5%88.

"Revolutions of 1989." Accessed August 2, 2021, https://en.wikipedia.org/wiki/Revolutions_of_1989#Hungary.

"Schönbrunn Palace." Accessed June 30, 2021, https://en.wikipedia.org/wiki/Sch%C3%B6nbrunn_Palace.

"Škoda Works." Accessed August 2, 2021, https://en.wikipedia.org/wiki/%C5%A0koda_Works#cite_note-2.

"Slovak National Party." Accessed August 2, 2021,

https://en.wikipedia.org/wiki/Slovak_National_Party.

"St. George's Basilica, Prague." Accessed August 1, 2021, https://en.wikipedia.org/wiki/St._George%27s_Basilica,_Prague.

"St. John the Baptist Cathedral (Trnava)." Accessed August 2, 2021, https://en.wikipedia.org/wiki/St._John_the_Baptist_Cathedral_(Trnava).

"St. Stephen's Cathedral, Vienna." Accessed June 30, 2021, https://en.wikipedia.org/wiki/St._Stephen%27s_Cathedral,_Vienna.

"St. Vitus Cathedral." Accessed August 1, 2021, https://en.wikipedia.org/wiki/St._Vitus_Cathedral.

"Trnava." Accessed August 2, 2021, https://en.wikipedia.org/wiki/Trnava.

"Velvet Revolution." Accessed August 1, 2021, https://en.wikipedia.org/wiki/Velvet_Revolution.

"Warsaw Pact invasion of Czechoslovakia." Accessed July 31, 2021, https://en.wikipedia.org/wiki/Warsaw_Pact_invasion_of_Czechoslovakia.

"Wenceslaus I, Duke of Bohemia." Accessed August 2, 2021, https://en.wikipedia.org/wiki/Wenceslaus_I,_Duke_of_Bohemia.

About the Author

Graduation with an MBA in 1992

After graduating in 1992 with a master in Business Administration from St. Cloud State University with honors, the author moved with her young daughters to Florida. At the time, she had been accepted by Old Dominion University for a doctorate study in International Marketing but turned it down in order to care for her younger children as she went through her divorce. After settling in the Tampa Bay area, she went through a training program to become a software engineer and worked for a major telecommunications company until she retired in 2017. She currently resides with her husband and attends First Christian Church in Venice, Florida.